Chanakya

Chanakya (350 – 275 BCE)was an Indian teacher, philosopher, and royal advisor.

Chanakya was born in a Brahmin family. Chanakya's birthplace is a matter of controversy, and there are multiple theories about his origin. According to the Buddhist text *Mahavamsa Tika*, his birthplace was Taxila.The Jain scriptures, such as *Adbidhana Chintamani*, mention him as a *Dramila*, implying that he was a native of South India. According to the Jainwriter Hemachandra's *Parishishtaparva*, Chanakya was born in the Canaka village of the Golla region, to a Brahmin named Canin and his wife Canesvari. Other sources mention his father's name as Chanak and state that Chanakya's name derives from his father's name. According to some sources, Chanakya was Brahmin from north India, scholar in Vedas, and a devotee of Lord Vishnu. According to Jain accounts he became Jain in old age like Chandragupta Maurya.

There is little purely historical information about Chanakya: most of it comes from semi-legendary accounts. Thomas Trautmann identifies four distinct accounts of the ancient Chanakya-Chandragupta *katha* (legend)

Version of the legend	Example texts
Buddhist version	*Mahavamsa* and its commentary *Vamsatthappakasini* (Pali language)
Jain version	*Parisistaparvan* by Hemachandra
Kashmiri version	*Kathasaritsagara* by Somadeva, *Brihat-Katha-Manjari* by Ksemendra
Vishakhadatta's version	*Mudrarakshasa*, a Sanskrit play by Vishakhadatta

The following elements are common to these legends:

The King Dhana Nanda insults Chanakya, prompting Chanakya to swear revenge and destroy the Nanda EmpireChanakya searches for one worthy successor to the Nanda and finds the young Chandragupta MauryaWith the help of some allies, Chanakya and Chandragupta bring down the Nanda empire, often using manipulative and secretive meansIdentification with Kautilya or Vishnugupta. The ancient treatise *Arthashastra* has been traditionally attributed to Chanakya by a number of scholars. The *Arthaśhāstra* identifies its author by the name Kautilya, except for one verse that refers to him by the name Vishnugupta. Kautilya is presumably the name of the author's gotra (clan).

One of the earliest Sanskrit literatures to identify Chanakya with Vishnugupta explicitly was Vishnu Sharma's *Panchatantra* in the 3rd century BCE.

K. C. Ojha puts forward the view that the traditional identification of Vishnugupta with Kautilya was caused by a confusion of the text's editor and its originator. He suggests that Vishnugupta was a redactor of the original work of Kautilya. Thomas Burrow goes even further and suggests that Chanakya and Kautilya may have been two different people.

Early life

Chanakya was educated at Takshashila, an ancient centre of learning located in north-western ancient India (present-day Pakistan). He later became a teacher (*acharya*) at the same place. Chanakya's life was connected to two cities: Takshashila and Pataliputra (present-day Patna in Bihar, India). Pataliputra was the capital of the Magadha kingdom, which was connected to Takshashila by Uttarapatha, the northern high road of commerce.

Role in the fall of the Nanda empire

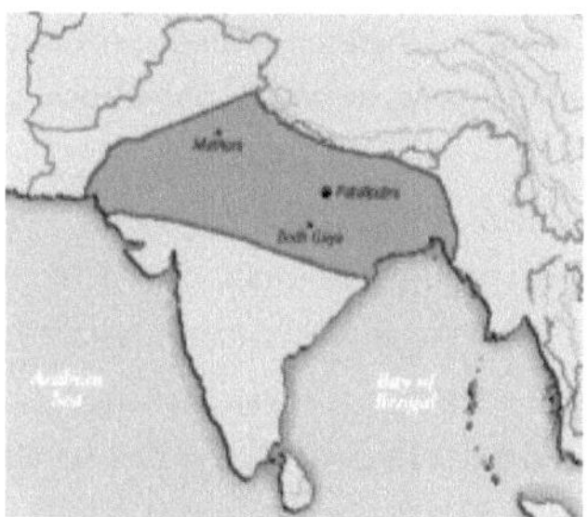

The Dhana Nanda, circa 323 BCE

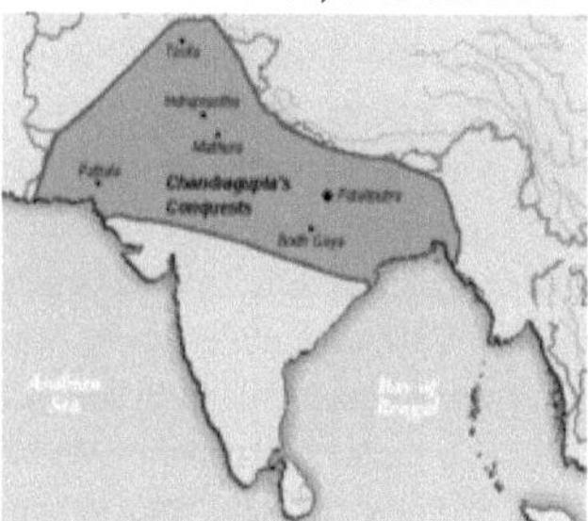

Chandragupta's empire in its early years

Chankaya and Chandragupta have been credited with defeating the powerful Nanda Empire and establishing the new Maurya Empire.

Mudrarakshasa ("The Signet of the Minister"), a play dated variously from the late 4th century to the early 8th century, narrates the ascent of Chandragupta Maurya to power: Sakatala, an unhappy royal minister, introduced Chanakya to the Nanda king, knowing that Chanakya would not be treated well in the court. Insulted at the court, Chanakya untied the sikha (lock of hair) and swore that he would not tie it back till he destroyed the Nanda kingdom. According to *Mudrarakshasa*, Chandragupta was the son of a royal concubine named Mura and spent his childhood in the Nanda palace. Chanakya and Chandragupta signed a pact with Parvataka (identified with King Porus by some scholars) of north-west India that ensured his victory over the Nanda empire. Kingdom of Nepal provided safe sanctuary to the followers of Chanakya during his operations.

Their combined army had Shaka, Yavana (Greek),Kirata, Kamboja and Vahlik soldiers. Following their victory, the territories of the Nanda empire were divided between Parvataka and Chanakya's associate Chandragupta.

However, after Parvataka's death, his son Malayaketu sought control of all the former Nanda territories. He was supported by Rakshasaa, the former Nanda minister, several of whose attempts to kill Chandragupta were foiled by Chanakya. As part of their game plan, Chanakya and Chandragupta faked a rift between themselves. As a sham, Chandragupta removed Chanakya from his ministerial post, while declaring that Rakshasa is better than him. Chanakya's agents in Malayaketu's court then turned the king against Rakshasa by suggesting that Rakshasa was poised to replace Chanakya in Chandragupta's court. The activities by Chanakya's spies further widened the rift between Malayaketu and Rakshasa. His agents also fooled Malayaketu into believing that five of his allies were planning to join Chandragupta, prompting Malayaketu to order their killings. In the end, Rakshasa ends up joining Chandragupta's side, and Malayaketu's coaliation is completely undone by Chanakya's strategy.

According to the Buddhist texts, Chandragupta was the son of the chief of the Moriya clan of Pippalivana. Chanakya once saw him leading a band of local youth and was highly impressed. He picked Chandragupta as the leader of the anti-Nanda revolt.[24]

Several modern adaptions of the legend narrate the story of Chanakya in a semi-fictional form, extending these legends. In *Chandragupta* (1911), a play by Dwijendralal Ray, the Nanda king exiles his half-brother Chandragupta, who joins the army of Alexander the Great. Later, with help from Chanakya and Katyayan (the former Prime Minister of Magadha), Chandragupta defeats Nanda, who is put to death by Chanakya.

Twenty-first-century works such as *Chanakya* (2001) by B. K. Chaturvedi and *Chanakya's Chant* (2010) by Ashwin Sanghi also present semi-fictional narratives of Chanakya's life. According to these, Chanakya's father Chanak was a friend of Shaktar, the Prime Minister of the Magadha kingdom, and Chanakya loved Shaktar's daughter Suvashini. Shaktar had lost much of his political clout to another courtier called Rakshasa, and one night, Shaktar was imprisoned by the King Dhana Nanda. The rivalry of the Chanakya's family with King Dhana Nanda started when Chanak openly criticised the misrule of the king. After the execution of Chanak by the King, the former Magadha minister Katyayan sent Chanakya to Acharya Pundarikaksha of Takshashila. Chanakya completed his education at Takshashila and became a teacher there. After some years, he returned to Pataliputra to meet his mother, only to learn that she was dead. He also learnt that the Nanda administration had further deteriorated under the growing influence of Rakshasa, who had made Suvashini his mistress. When Chanakya visited the royal court to advise him, he was insulted and imprisoned by the king. Chanakya was rescued by the men of General Maurya, another person who despised with the king's rule. Chanakya took Chandragupta Maurya to Takshashila, where he trained the young man. King Ambhi, the ruler of Takshashila, had allied with the invader Alexander the Great to defeat Parvataka. Chanakya and Chandragupta gathered a band of people discontented with Ambhi's rule and formed an alliance with Parvataka to defeat the Nanda king. Their initial attempts at conquering Magadha were unsuccessful. Once, Chanakya came across a mother scolding her child for burning himself by eating from the middle of a bowl of porridge rather than the cooler edge. Chanakya realized his initial strategic error: he was attacking Magadha, the center of the Nanda territory. He then changed his strategy and focused on capturing the areas located at the peripharies of the Nanda empire. With help from Suvashini, he drove a wedge between the king and Rakshasa. Finally, he defeated the last Nanda king and established a new empire with Chandragupta Maurya as the emperor.

After the establishment of the Maurya EmpireSilver punch mark coin of the Maurya Empire, with symbols of wheel and elephant, 3rd century BCE. Chanakya continued to serve as an advisor to Chandragupta after the establishment of the Maurya Empire. According to a popular legend mentioned in the Jain texts, Chanakya used to add small doses of poison to the food eaten by Emperor Chandragupta Maurya (mithridatism) in order to make him immune to the poisoning attempts by the enemies. Unaware, Chandragupta once fed some of his food to his queen, Durdhara, who was seven days away from delivery. The queen, not immune to the poison, collapsed and died within a few minutes. In order to save the heir to the throne, Chanakya cut the queen's belly open and extracted the foetus just as she died. The baby was namedBindusara, because he was touched by a drop (*bindu*) of blood having poison.

When Bindusara was in his youth, Chandragupta gave up the throne and followed the Jain saint Bhadrabahu to present day Karnataka and settled in the place of Shravana Belagola. He lived as an ascetic for some years and died of voluntary starvation according to Jain tradition. Chanakya meanwhile stayed in the court as an advisor to Bindusara.

Death

According to one legend, Chanakya retired to the jungle and starved himself to death. According to another legend mentioned by the Jain writer Hemachandra, Chanakya died as a result of a conspiracy by Subandhu, one of Bindusara's ministers. Subandhu, who did not like Chanakya, told Bindusara that Chanakya was responsible for the murder of his mother. Bindusara asked the nurses, who confirmed the story of his birth. Bindusara was horrified and enraged. When Chanakya, who was an old man by this time, learned that the King was angry with him, he decided to end his life. In accordance with the Jain tradition, he decided to starve himself to death. By this time, the King had found out the full story: Chanakya was not directly responsible for his mother's death, which was an accident. He asked Subandhu to convince Chanakya to give up his plan to kill himself. However, Subandhu, pretending to conduct a ceremony for Chanakya, burned Chanakya alive.

Literary works

Two books are attributed to Chanakya: *Arthashastra* and *Chanakya Niti*, also known as *Chanakya Neeti-shastra*.[34]

The *Arthashastra* discusses monetary and fiscal policies, wel fare, international relations, and war strategies in detail. The text also outlines the duties of a ruler. Some scholars believe that *Arthashastra* is actually a compilation of a number of earlier texts written by various authors, and Chanakya might have been *one* of these authors.

Chanakya Niti is a collection of aphorisms, said to be selected by Chanakya from the various shastras.[34]

Legacy

Arthashastra is serious manual on statecraft, on how to run a state, informed by a higher purpose, clear and precise in its prescriptions, the result of practical experience of running a state. It is not just a normative text but a realist description of the art of running a state.

Chanakya is regarded as a great thinker and diplomat in India. Many Indian nationalists regard him as one of the earliest people who envisaged the united India spanning the entire subcontinent. India's former National Security Advisor Shiv Shankar Menon praised Chanakya's Arthashastra for its clear and precise rules which apply even today. Furthermore, he recommended reading of the book for broadening the vision on strategic issues.

The diplomatic enclave in New Delhi is named Chanakyapuri in honour of Chanakya. Institutes named after him include Training Ship Chanakya, Chanakya National Law University and Chanakya Institute of Public Leadership. Chanakya circle in Mysore has been named after him.

Originally a professor of economics and political science at the ancient Takshashila University, Chanakya managed the first Maurya Emperor Chandragupta's rise to power at a young age. He is widely credited for having played an important role in the establishment of the Maurya Empire, which was the first empire in archaeologically recorded history to rule most of the Indian subcontinent. Chanakya served as the chief advisor to both Chandragupta and his son Bindusara.

Chanakya is traditionally identified as **Kautilya** or **Vishnu Gupta**, who authored the ancient Indian political treatise called *Arthasastra* (*Economics*). As such, he is considered as the pioneer of the field of political science and economics in India, and his work is thought of as an important precursor to classical economics. His works were lost near the end of the Gupta dynasty and not rediscovered until 1915.

Kautilya Management Consultants is an 8 yrs old ERA accredited recruitment firm. Kautilya Management Consultants derives its name from the historical figure Chanakya (also known as Kautilya), one of the worlds first management gurus who lived in 4th century BC. He was credited with having identified the leadership qualities in a young kid Chandragupta Maurya and nurtured him to become the first emperor of India. Our philosophy is to be the strategic and cost effective business partner of choice for recruitments and allied services.We have partnered with fortune 500 MNCs, large Indian corporates, start ups and emerging companies for their recruitments and staffing needs across levels and domains.

The fall of the Magadha & the rise of the mauryan dynasty

At the time of Kautilya, India was mostly composed of a number of small independent states, with the exception of the

Magadha kingdom, a realm that controlled most of Northern India, which was ruled by the Nanda dynasty. The fame of Kautilya is owed to the important role he played in the fall of the Magadha kingdom and the rise to power of the Mauryan dynasty. In order to accomplish this, he became an ally and loyal servant of Chandragupta, a noble member of the Kshatriya caste (the warrior ruler's caste) who was related to the Nanda family, but he was an exile. Before he became Chandragupta's ally, Kautilya was introduced to the Nanda king, who insulted him. Kautilya untied his sikha (lock of hair on male Hindus), and swore he would only tie it back once the Nanda dynasty was destroyed.

There are a number of accounts concerning kautilya which describe him as both intelligent and ruthless.

Kautilya and Chandragupta raised a small army that lacked sufficient military strength to take the Magadha throne directly. Therefore, Kautilya's cunning strategies became useful: Chandragupta entered the capital of the Magadha kingdom, Pataliputra, where he triggered a civil **war** using Kautilya Chanakya's intelligence network. In 322 BCE Chandragupta finally seized the throne putting an end to the Nanda dynasty and he established the Mauryan dynasty which would rule India until 185 BCE. After this victory, Chandragupta fought and defeated the generals of**Alexander the Great** located in Gandhara, present day Afghanistan. Following these successful campaigns, Chandragupta was seen as a brave leader who defeated part of the **Greek** invaders and ended the corrupt Nanda government and thus gained wide public support.

There are a number of accounts concerning Kautilya which describe him as both intelligent and ruthless. One of these accounts tells us that once the last Nanda was defeated and the imperial palace was occupied by the new Mauryan dynasty, Kautilya noticed a group of ants carrying grain out of a crack in the palace floor. After examining the crack he discovered hordes of Nanda soldiers in a basement below, ready for a surprise attack. Emotionless, Kautilya emptied the building leaving the Nanda soldiers locked up, and burnt the palace to the ground. It is also said that when the Nanda king was killed, Kautilya personally went to see the body and, just before tying up his hair, he ordered the body to remain uncremated, to discard it and turn it into carrion. This was a truly barbaric end and contrary to Indian tradition for any deceased and the highest insult for a man's immortal soul.

Kautilya helped Chandragupta to turn the Mauryan Empire into one of the most powerful governments at that time. Pataliputra remained as the imperial capital and the initial territory controlled by Chandragupta extended all across Northern India from the Indus river in the west to the Bay of Bengal in the East. Later on in 305 BCE, the Mauryan Empire gained control of the Punjab, what today is part of Northern India and Eastern Pakistan, an area that had been controlled by the Macedonians.

Mauryan Ringstone

The political thoughts of Kautilya are summarized in a book he wrote known as the ***Arthashastra***, a Sanskrit name which is translated as "The Science of Material Gain". This book was lost for many centuries and a copy of it written on palm leaves was rediscovered in India in 1904 CE. The *Arthashastra* is a handbook for running an empire effectively and it contains detailed information about specific topics. Diplomacy and war are the two points treated in greater detail than any other and it also includes recommendations on law, prisons, taxation, fortifications, **coinage**, manufacturing, **trade**, administrations, and spies.

The ideas expressed by Kautilya in the *Arthashastra* are totally practical and unsentimental. Kautliya openly writes about controversial topics such as assassinations, when to kill family members, how to manage secret agents, when it is useful to violate treaties and when to spy on ministers. Because of this, Kautilya is often compared to Machiavelli. It is fair to mention that Kautilya is not merciless all the time and he also writes about the moral duty of the king: he summarizes the duty of the king by saying "The happiness of the subjects is the happiness of the king; their welfare is his. His own pleasure is not his good but the pleasure of his subjects is his good". Some scholars have seen in the ideas of Kautilya a combination of Chinese **Confucianism** and Legalism.

Death & Legacy

How Kautilya died is not entirely clear. Some accounts say he starved himself to death, a common practice in**Jainism**. Other versions say he died as a result of a court conspiracy. What we know for sure is that his death took place when Bindusara, the second Mauryan ruler, was on the throne. Kautilya was a pioneer in diplomacy and government administration. His merit was not only to come up with very important practical advice for government, but also to organize them in a systematic and logical fashion. Even today, the *Arthashastra* is the number one classic of diplomacy in India. His vision of a unified India would become a reality during the time of **Ashoka**, the third ruler of the Mauryan dynasty.

My Views on Kautilya

Kautilya, also called **Chanakya** or **Vishnugupta** (flourished 300 BCE), Hindu statesman and philosopher who wrote a classic treatise on polity, *Artha-shastra*("The Science of Material Gain"), a compilation of almost everything that had been written in India up to his time regarding *artha* (property, economics, or material success).

He was born into a Brahman family and received his education at Taxila (now in Pakistan). He is known to have had a knowledge of medicine and astrology, and it is believed he was familiar with elements of Greek and Persian learning introduced into India by Zoroastrians. Some authorities believe he was a Zoroastrian or at least was strongly influenced by that religion.

Kautilya became a counselor and adviser to Chandragupta (reigned *c.* 321–*c.* 297), founder of the Mauryan empire of northern India, but lived by himself. He was instrumental in helping Chandragupta overthrow the powerful Nanda dynasty at Pataliputra, in the Magadha region.

Kautilya's book came to be Chandragupta's guide. Each of its 15 sections deals with a phase of government, which Kautilya sums up as "the science of punishment." He openly advises the development of an elaborate spy system reaching into all levels of society and encourages political and secret assassination. Lost for centuries, the book was discovered in 1905.

Compared by many to Italian statesman and writer Niccolò Machiavelli and by others to Aristotle and Plato, Kautilya is alternately condemned for his ruthlessness and trickery and praised for his sound political wisdom and knowledge of human nature. All authorities agree, however, that it was mainly because of Kautilya that the Mauryan empire under Chandragupta and later under Ashoka (reigned *c.* 265–*c.* 238) became a model of efficient government.

Kautilya and *Arthashastra*

Much of our knowledge about state policy under the Mauryas comes from the *Arthashastra* written by Kautilya (more popularly known as Chanakya), who was a Brahmin minister under Chandragupta Maurya. Though it was written at the end of the fourth century BC, it appears to have been rediscovered only in 1905, after centuries of oblivion. The treatise in its present form is most likely not the text written by Kautilya, though it is probably based on a text that was authored by Kautilya; and in no case can the text in its entirety be ascribed to Kautilya, on account of numerous stylistic and linguistic variations.

The book, written in Sanskrit, discusses theories and principles of governing a state. It is not an account of Mauryan administration. The title,*Arthashastra*, which means "the Science of Material Gain" or "Science of Polity", does not leave any doubts about its ends. According to Kautilya, the ruler should use any means to attain his goal and his actions required no moral sanction. The only problems discussed are of the most practical kind. Though the kings were allowed a free rein, the citizens were subject to a rigid set of rules. This double standard has been cited as an excuse for the obsolescence of the *Arthashastra*, though the real cause of its ultimate neglect, as the Indian historian Romila Thapar suggests, was the formation of a totally different society to which these methods no longer applied.

Arthashastra remains unique in all of Indian literature because of its total absence of specious reasoning, or its unabashed advocacy of realpolitik, and scholars continued to study it for its clear cut arguments and formal prose till the twelfth century. Espionage and the liberal use of provocative agents is recommended on a large scale. Murder and false accusations were to be used by a king's secret agents without any thoughts to morals or ethics. There are chapters for kings to help them keep in check the premature ambitions of their sons, and likewise chapters intended to help princes to thwart their fathers' domineering authority. However, Kautilya ruefully admits that it is just as difficult to detect an official's dishonesty as it is to discover how much water is drunk by the swimming fish.

Kautilya helped the young Chandragupta Maurya, who was a Vaishya, to ascend to the Nanda throne in 321 BC. Kautilya's counsel is particularly remarkable because the young Maurya's supporters were not as well armed as the Nandas. Kautilya continued to help Chandragupta Maurya in his campaigns and his influence was crucial in consolidating the great Mauryan empire. He has often been likened to Machiavelli by political theorists, and the name of

Chanakya is still reminiscent of a vastly scheming and clever political adviser. In very recent years, Indian state television, or *Doordarshan* as it is known, commissioned and screened a television serial on the life and intrigues of Chanakya.

It is customary on such occasions to say how delighted one is to come to a meeting and how appropriate its subject is. Today, for once, I mean it in full measure. I am truly delighted to be here at the workshop on Kautilya organised by the IDSA. I must congratulate Director Arvind Gupta on this initiative.

1. On Reading Kautilya Again

The *Arthashastra* meets one essential criterion for a great book. It bears reading again and again. Every time you read it you learn something new and find a new way of looking at events. But it is a very different sort of text from the *Bhagwad Gita*. This is not a book that you keep on your bedside table and turn to for daily inspiration. This is a serious manual on statecraft, on how to run a state, informed by a higher purpose (or *dharma*), clear and precise in its prescriptions, the result of practical experience of running a state. It is not just a normative text but a realist description of the art of running a state.

Reading the text again now, I was struck by how evidently Kautilya himself, (if indeed the author of the *Arthashastra* was one man and not a historical composite), is clearly the product of centuries of evolved strategic thinking. He cites several previous authorities differing views on many issues. Bharadvaja, Vishalaksha, Parasara, Pisuna and others are mentioned often. Kautilya argues with them, while presenting their views before his own. Sadly, what we know of many of them is limited to what Kautilya tells us.

Equally, Kautilya's is only one voice, and the Arthashastra is probably meant to be a normative text, describing how the state should work. Ashoka's imagining of the state's place in the world, judging by his inscriptions, and his practice do not bear out what the Arthashastra says. Other Indian texts have different points of view, for instance the Buddhist Nikaya texts, on statecraft and defence. The Arthashastra and Kautilya are therefore one of several approaches to statecraft in Ancient India. It is also a text of its time and place, Mauryan to Gupta administration, and should be read as such.

2. Reconnecting with Indian Strategic Thought

We are afflicted with neglect of our pre-modern histories, and many of us believe orientalist caricatures of India. India's supposedly incoherent strategic approach is actually a colonial construct, as is the idea of Indians somehow forgetting their own history and needing to be taught it by Westerners who retrieved it. The version that they "retrieved" was a construct that was useful to perpetuate colonial rule and, after independence, to induce self-doubt and a willingness to follow.

Reading Kautilya and the other indigenous texts is one way to give the lie to these theories.

The other is to consider strategic practice in India over the ages. One only has to think of the Mahabharata, (our own Warring States period slightly later), the histories of the Deccan, Kerala, and Bundelkhand in medieval times, (to pick a few examples at random), and what we have undergone in the sixty-five years since independence, to see continuity in Indian strategic practice. Fortunately younger Indian historians are now working on these subjects with unblinkered minds. I have just read a book by Jayashree Vivekanandan called Interrogating International Relations (Routledge, 2011) which analyses Mughal grand strategy. It strengthened my faith that our scholarly tradition is alive.

But as a general rule, today our theory has yet to catch up with our rich historical praxis.

Reading Kautilya (and other texts like the *Shantiparva* of the Mahabharata) one is reminded that this was not always so. One is also reminded of the rich experience in our tradition of multipolarity, of asymmetries in the distribution of power, of debate on the purposes of power (where *dharma* is defined), of the utility of force, and of several other issues with contemporary resonance. In many ways it is India's historical experience of poly-centric multistate systems, plurality, and of the omni-directional diplomacy and relativistic statecraft that it produced, that is closer to the world we see today. (In contrast, the single-sovereign, universalist, and hierarchical statecraft and diplomacy of traditional China is easier to explain and attractive in its simplicity but fundamentally different.)

Let me be clear. I am not trying to idealize the Indian past. There is a risk here that the analytic tradition becomes the historical tradition, that we confuse cause and effect, and that imageries become the reality that they were intended to reflect. All I am saying is that some of the problems in IR and strategic studies that we think we are dealing with for the first time have been considered by great minds in India before. We are the poorer for ignoring them. We can, instead, use the past to learn ways of thinking about these problems, improving our mental discipline, as it were.

Besides, states behave in ways that cannot be entirely explained by rational calculation or logic. (If they were they would be predictable.) Studying strategic traditions and cultures gives us a better understanding of why this is so. And where better to start than with oneself. A little self-awareness cannot hurt.

Let me give you an example of what I mean. When we in India call for a plural, inclusive and open security architecture in the Indo-Pacific we are well within a tradition and culture of thought which was relativistic, idea driven and omni-directional. Other traditions, which are more hierarchical, claiming universal validity, find these ideas hard to understand. (And we are shocked when they do not espouse what to us are our eminently sensible views!) Friends tell me that Chola, Pandyan and Oriya manuscripts and inscriptions are early examples of what the free flow of goods, ideas and people could achieve -- the ancient version of the open, inclusive architecture that we speak of today.

3. Creating our Own Modern Strategic Vocabulary

Some of you will groan and say, "There he goes again on his hobby horse". But let me explain why this is important.

To be honest among ourselves, much of what passes for strategic thinking in India today is derivative, using concepts, doctrines and a vocabulary derived from other cultures, times, places and conditions. This is why, with a few honorable exceptions like the home-grown nuclear doctrine, it fails to serve our needs, impact policy, or to find a place in domestic and international discourse.

Jawaharlal Nehru made a beginning towards creating modern Indian strategic thought. But his work was incomplete, even though it was taken forward and developed by others like K Subrahmaniam. Besides, the world has evolved rapidly since Nehru's time.

There is also no question that we live in a world that is different from Kautilya's in terms of technology and experience,. But human responses are still similar, as is the behaviour of the states that humans create and run. That is why reading Kautilya helps us by broadening our vision on issues of strategy.

It will, naturally, take time and practice for us to develop our own strategic vocabulary and doctrines. This will require patience, but must be done if India is to truly seek the broadest possible degree of strategic autonomy. After all autonomy begins in the mind. As I said earlier, fortunately the younger generation of Indian scholars shows signs of doing the necessary work and are thinking for themselves.

Strategic doctrines and cultures are not built in a day. I was, therefore, happy to see that this workshop is part of a broader Indigenous Historical Knowledge project by the IDSA. May I also suggest that this workshop be the first of a series that builds upon the beginning that you are making here? I assume that future workshops and work in the project on Indigenous Historical Knowledge will also cover other Indian thinkers and themes.

The Arthashastra by Kautilya

Kautilya (also Chanakya) was the chief adviser of Chandragupta Maurya. The Arthasastra by Kautilya is another important source which throws a good deal of light on the Mauryan period. As Kautilya (or Chanakya), was directly concerned with the Mauryan government, his book gives a very valuable information regarding the political condition of India during the Mauryan period arid the Mauryan administration.

Arthashastra is a unique book on the subject of politics and art of government in the literature of ancient India. This book is a huge work and has fifteen parts, each dealing with some aspects of the art of government.

Kautilya's *Arthashastra*: The Duties of Government Superintendents

I. FORMATION OF VILLAGES.

EITHER by inducing foreigners to immigrate (*paradesapraváhanena*) or by causing the thickly-populated centres of his own kingdom to send forth the excessive population (*svadésábhishyandavámanéna vá*), the king may construct villages either on new sites or on old ruins (*bhútapúrvama vá*).

Villages consisting each of not less than a hundred families and of not more than five-hundred families of agricultural people of *súdra* caste, with boundaries extending as far as a *krósa* (2250 yds.) or two, and capable of protecting each other shall be formed. Boundaries shall be denoted by a river, a mountain, forests, bulbous plants (*grishti*), caves, artificial buildings (*sétubandha*), or by trees such as *sálmali* (silk cotton tree), samí (*Acacia Suma*), and kshíravriksha (milky trees).

There shall be set up a *stháníya* (a fortress of that name) in the centre of eight-hundred villages, a drónamukha in the centre of four-hundred villages, a khárvátika in the centre of two-hundred villages and sangrahana in the midst of a collection of ten villages.

There shall be constructed in the extremities of the kingdom forts manned by boundary-guards (*antapála*) whose duty shall be to guard the entrances into the kingdom. The interior of the kingdom shall be watched by trap-keepers (*vágurika*), archers (*sábara*), hunters (*pulinda*), chandálas, and wild tribes (*aranyachára*).

Those who perform sacrifices (*ritvik*), spiritual guides, priests, and those learned in the Vedas shall be granted Brahmadaya lands yielding sufficient produce and exempted from taxes and fines (*adandkaráni*).

Superintendents, Accountants, Gopas, Sthánikas, Veterinary Surgeons (*Aníkastha*), physicians, horse-trainers, and messengers shall also be endowed with lands which they shall have no right to alienate by sale or mortgage.

Lands prepared for cultivation shall be given to tax- payers (*karada*) only for life (*ekapurushikáni*).

Unprepared lands shall not be taken away from those who are preparing them for cultivation.

Lands may be confiscated from those who do not cultivate them; and given to others; or they may be cultivated by village labourers (*grámabhritaka*) and traders (*vaidehaka*), lest those owners who do not properly cultivate them might pay less (to the government). If cultivators pay their taxes easily, they may be favourably supplied with grains, cattle, and money.

The king shall bestow on cultivators only such favour and remission (*anugrahapariharau*) as will tend to swell the treasury, and shall avoid such as will deplete it.

A king with depleted treasury will eat into the very vitality of both citizens and country people. Either on the occasion of opening new settlements or on any other emergent occasions, remission of taxes shall be made.

He shall regard with fatherly kindness those who have passed the period of remission of taxes.

He shall carry on mining operations and manufactures, exploit timber and elephant forests, offer facilities for cattlebreeding and commerce, construct roads for traffic both by land and water, and set up market towns (*panyapattana*).

He shall also construct reservoirs (*sétu*) filled with water either perennial or drawn from some other source. Or he may provide with sites, roads, timber, and other necessary things those who construct reservoirs of their own accord. Likewise in the construction of places of pilgrimage (*punyasthána*) and of groves.

Whoever stays away from any kind of cooperative construction (*sambhúya setubhandhát*) shall send his servants and bullocks to carry on his work, shall have a share in the expenditure, but shall have no claim to the profit.

The king shall exercise his right of ownership (*swámyam*) with regard to fishing, ferrying and trading in vegetables (*haritapanya*) in reservoirs or lakes (*sétushu*).

Those who do not heed the claims of their slaves (*dása*), hirelings (*áhitaka*), and relatives shall be taught their duty.

The king shall provide the orphans, (*bála*), the aged, the infirm, the afflicted, and the helpless with maintenance. He shall also provide subsistence to helpless women when they are carrying and also to the children they give birth to.

Elders among the villagers shall improve the property of bereaved minors till the latter attain their age; so also the property of Gods.

When a capable person other than an apostate (*patita*) or mother neglects to maintain his or her child, wife, mother, father, minor brothers, sisters, or widowed girls (*kanyá vidhaváscha*), he or she shall be punished with a fine of twelve panas.

When, without making provision for the maintenance of his wife and sons, any person embraces ascetism, he shall be punished with the first amercement; likewise any person who converts a woman to ascetism (*pravrájayatah*).

Whoever has passed the age of copulation may become an ascetic after distributing the properties of his own acquisition (among his sons); otherwise, he will be punished.

No ascetic other than a *vánaprastha* (forest-hermit), no company other than the one of local birth (*sajátádanyassanghah*), and no guilds of any kind other than local cooperative guilds (*sámuttháyiká- danyassamayánubandhah*) shall find entrance into the villages of the kingdom. Nor shall there be in villages buildings (*sáláh*) intended for sports and plays. Nor, in view of procuring money, free labour, commodities, grains, and liquids in plenty, shall actors, dancers, singers, drummers, buffoons (*vágjívana*), and bards (*kusílava*) make any disturbance to the work of the villagers; for helpless villagers are always dependent and bent upon their fields.

The king shall avoid taking possession of any country which is liable to the inroads of enemies and wild tribes and which is harassed by frequent visitations of famine and pestilence. He shall also keep away from expensive sports.He shall protect agriculture from the molestation of oppressive fines, free labour, and taxes (*dandavishtikarábádhaih*); herds of cattle from thieves, tigers, poisonous creatures and cattle-disease.

He shall not only clear roads of traffic from the molestations of courtiers (*vallabha*), of workmen (*kármika*), of robbers, and of boundary-guards, but also keep them from being destroyed by herds of cattle.

Thus the king shall not only keep in good repair timber and elephant forests, buildings, and mines created in the past, but also set up new ones.

II. DIVISION **OF LAND**

THE King shall make provision for pasture grounds on uncultivable tracts.

Bráhmans shall be provided with forests for sóma plantation, for religious learning, and for the performance of penance, such forests being rendered safe from the dangers from animate or inanimate objects, and being named after the tribal name (*gótra*) of the Bráhmans resident therein.

A forest as extensive as the above, provided with only one entrance rendered inaccessible by the construction of ditches all round, with plantations of delicious fruit trees, bushes, bowers, and thornless trees, with an expansive lake of water full of harmless animals, and with tigers (*vyála*), beasts of prey (*márgáyuka*), male and female elephants, young elephants, and bisons—all deprived of their claws and teeth—shall be formed for the king's sports.

On the extreme limit of the country or in any other suitable locality, another game-forest with game-beasts; open to all, shall also be made. In view of procuring all kinds of forest-produce described elsewhere, one or several forests shall be specially reserved.

Manufactories to prepare commodities from forest produce shall also be set up.

Wild tracts shall be separated from timber-forests. In the extreme limit of the country, elephant forests, separated from wild tracts, shall be formed.

The superintendent of forests with his retinue of forest guards shall not only maintain the up-keep of the forests, but also acquaint himself with all passages for entrance into, or exit from such of them as are mountainous or boggy or contain rivers or lakes.

Whoever kills an elephant shall be put to death.

Whoever brings in the pair of tusks of an elephant, dead from natural causes, shall receive a reward of four-and-a-half panas.

Guards of elephant forests, assisted by those who rear elephants, those who enchain the legs of elephants, those who guard the boundaries, those who live in forests, as well as by those who nurse elephants, shall, with the help of five or seven female elephants to help in tethering wild ones, trace the whereabouts of herds of elephants by following the course of urine and dungs left by elephants and along forest-tracts covered over with branches of Bhallátaki (*Semicarpus Anacardium*), and by observing the spots where elephants slept or sat before or left dungs, or where they had just destroyed the banks of rivers or lakes. They shall also precisely ascertain whether any mark is due to the movements of elephants in herds, of an elephant roaming single, of a stray elephant, of a leader of herds, of a tusker, of a rogue elephant, of an elephant in rut, of a young elephant, or of an elephant that has escaped from the cage.

Experts in catching elephants shall follow the instructions given to them by the elephant doctor (*aníkastha*) and catch such elephants as are possessed of auspicious characteristics and good character.

The victory of kings (in battles) depends mainly upon elephants; for elephants, being of large bodily frame, are capable not only to destroy the arrayed army of an enemy, his fortifications, and encampments, but also to undertake works that are dangerous to life.

Elephants bred in countries, such as Kálinga, Anga, Karúsa, and the East are the best; those of the Dasárna and western countries are of middle quality; and those of Sauráshtra and Panchajana countries are of low quality. The might and energy of all can, however, be improved by suitable training.

III. CONSTRUCTION OF FORTS

ON all the four quarters of the boundaries of the kingdom, defensive fortifications against an enemy in war shall be constructed on grounds best fitted for the purpose: a water-fortification (*audaka*) such as an island in the midst of a river, or a plain surrounded by low ground; a mountainous fortification (*párvata*) such as a rocky tract or a cave; a desert (*dhánvana*) such as a wild tract devoid of water and overgrown with thicket growing in barren soil; or a forest fortification (*vanadurga*) full of wagtail (*khajana*), water and thickets.

Of these, water and mountain fortifications are best suited to defend populous centres; and desert and forest fortifications are habitations in wilderness (*atavísthánam*). Or with ready preparations for flight the king may have his fortified capital (*sthániya*) as the seat of his sovereignty (*samudayásthánam*) in the centre of his kingdom: in a locality naturally best fitted for the purpose, such as the bank of the confluence of rivers, a deep pool of perennial water, or of a lake or tank, a fort, circular, rectangular, or square in form, surrounded with an artificial canal of water, and connected with both land and water paths (may be constructed).

Round this fort, three ditches with an intermediate space of one danda (6 ft.) from each other, fourteen, twelve and ten dandas respectively in width, with depth less by one quarter or by one-half of their width, square at their bottom and one-third as wide as at their top, with sides built of stones or bricks, filled with perennial flowing water or with water drawn from some other source, and possessing crocodiles and lotus plants shall be constructed.

At a distance of four dandas (24 ft.) from the (innermost) ditch, a rampart six dandas high and twice as much broad shall be erected by heaping mud upwards and by making it square at the bottom, oval at the centre pressed by the trampling of elephants and bulls, and planted with thorny and poisonous plants in bushes. Gaps in the rampart shall be filled up with fresh earth.

Above the rampart, parapets in odd or even numbers and with an intermediate, space of from 12 to 24 hastas from each other shall be built of bricks and raised to a height of twice their breadth.

The passage for chariots shall be made of trunks of palm trees or of broad and thick slabs of stones with spheres like the head of a monkey carved on their surface; but never of wood as fire finds a happy abode in it.

Towers, square throughout and with moveable staircase or ladder equal to its height, shall also be constructed.

In the intermediate space measuring thirty dandas between two towers, there shall be formed a broad street in two compartments covered over with a roof and two-and- half times as long as it is broad.

Between the tower and the broad street there shall be constructed an Indrakósa which is made up of covering pieces of wooden planks affording seats for three archers.

There shall also be made a road for Gods which shall measure two hastas inside (the towers?), four times as much by the sides, and eight hastas along the parapet.

Paths (*chárya*, to ascend the parapet?) as broad as a danda (6 ft.) or two shall also be made.

In an unassailable part (of the rampart), a passage for flight (*pradhávitikám*), and a door for exit (*nishkuradwáram*) shall be made.

Outside the rampart, passages for movements shall be closed by forming obstructions such as a knee-breaker (*jánubhanjaní*), a trident, mounds of earth, pits, wreaths of thorns, instruments made like the tail of a snake, palm leaf, triangle, and of dog's teeth, rods, ditches filled with thorns and covered with sand, frying pans and water-pools.

Having made on both sides of the rampart a circular hole of a danda-and-a-half in diametre, an entrance gate (to the fort) one-sixth as broad as the width of the street shall be fixed.

A square (*chaturásra*) is formed by successive addition of one danda up to eight dandas commencing from five, or in the proportion, one-sixth of the length up to one-eighth.

The rise in level (*talotsedhah*) shall be made by successive addition of one hasta up to 18 hastas commencing from 15 hastas.

In fixing a pillar, six parts are to form its height, on the floor, twice as much (12 parts) to be entered into the ground, and one-fourth for its capital.

Of the first floor, five parts (are to be taken) for the formation of a hall (*sálá*), a well, and a boundary-house; two-tenths of it for the formation of two platforms opposite to each other (*pratimanchau*); an upper storey twice as high as its width; carvings of images; an upper-most storey, half or three-fourths as broad as the first floor; side walls built of bricks; on the left side, a staircase circumambulating from left to right; on the right, a secret staircase hidden in the wall; a top-support of ornamental arches (*toranasirah*) projecting as far as two hastas; two door-panels, (each) occupying three-fourths of the space; two and two cross-bars (*parigha*, to fasten the door); an iron-bolt (*indrakila*) as long as an aratni (24 angulas); a boundary gate (*ánidváram*) five hastas in width; four beams to shut the door against elephants; and turrets (*hastinakha*) (outside the rampart) raised up to the height of the face of a man, removable or irremovable, or made of earth in places devoid of water.

A turret above the gate and starting from the top of the parapet shall be constructed, its front resembling an alligator up to three-fourths of its height.

In the centre of the parapets, there shall be constructed a deep lotus pool; a rectangular building of four compartments, one within the other; an abode of the Goddess Kumiri (*Kumárípuram*), having its external area one-and-a-half times as broad as that of its innermost room; a circular building with an arch way; and in accordance with available space and materials, there shall also be constructed canals (*kulyá*) to hold weapons and three times as long as broad.

In those canals, there shall be collected stones, spades (*kuddála*), axes (*kuthári*), varieties of staffs, cudgel (*musrinthi*), hammers (*mudgara*), clubs, discus, machines (*yantra*), and such weapons as can destroy a hundred persons at once (*sataghni*), together with spears, tridents, bamboo-sticks with pointed edges made of iron, camel-necks, explosives (*agnisamyógas*), and whatever else can be devised and formed from available materials.

IV. BUILDINGS WITHIN THE FORT.

DEMARCATION of the ground inside the fort shall be made first by opening three royal roads from west to east and three from south to north.

The fort shall contain twelve gates, provided with both a land and water-way kept secret.

Chariot-roads, royal roads, and roads leading to drónamukha, stháníya, country parts, and pasture grounds shall each be four dandas (24 ft.) in width.

Roads leading to sayóníya (?), military stations (*vyúha*), burial or cremation grounds, and to villages shall be eight dandas in width.

Roads to gardens, groves, and forests shall be four dandas.

Roads leading to elephant forests shall be two dandas.

Roads for chariots shall be five aratnis (7½ ft.). Roads for cattle shall measure four aratnis; and roads for minor quadrupeds and men two aratnis.

Royal buildings shall be constructed on strong grounds.

In the midst of the houses of the people of all the four castes and to the north from the centre of the ground inside the fort, the king's palace, facing either the north or the east shall, as described elsewhere (Chapter XX, Book I), be constructed occupying one-ninth of the whole site inside the fort.

Royal teachers, priests, sacrificial place, water-reservoir and ministers shall occupy sites east by north to the palace.

Royal kitchen, elephant stables, and the store-house shall be situated on sites east by south.

On the eastern side, merchants trading in scents, garlands, grains, and liquids, together with expert artisans and the people of Kshatriya caste shall have their habitations.

The treasury, the accountant's office, and various manufactories (*karmanishadyáscha*) shall be situated on sites south by east.

The store-house of forest produce and the arsenal shall be constructed on sites south by west.

To the south, the superintendents of the city, of commerce, of manufactories, and of the army as well as those who trade in cooked rice, liquor, and flesh, besides prostitutes, musicians, and the people of Vaisya caste shall live.

To the west by south, stables of asses, camels, and working house.

To the west by north, stables of conveyances and chariots.

To the west, artisans manufacturing worsted threads, cotton threads, bamboo-mats, skins, armours, weapons, and gloves as well as the people of Súdra caste shall have their dwellings.

To the north by west, shops and hospitals.

To the north by east, the treasury and the stables of cows and horses.

To the north, the royal tutelary deity of the city, ironsmiths, artisans working on precious stones, as well as Bráhmans shall reside.

In the several corners, guilds and corporations of workmen shall reside.

In the centre of the city, the apartments of Gods such as Aparájita, Apratihata, Jayanta, Vaijayanta, Siva, Vaisravana, Asvina (divine physicians), and the honourable liquor-house (*Srí-madiragriham*), shall be situated.

In the corners, the guardian deities of the ground shall be appropriately set up.

Likewise the principal gates such as Bráhma, Aindra, Yámya, and Sainápatya shall be constructed; and at a distance of 100 bows (dhanus = 108 angulas) from the ditch (on the counterscarp side), places of worship and pilgrimage, groves and buildings shall be constructed.

Guardian deities of all quarters shall also be set up in quarters appropriate to them.

Either to the north or the east, burial or cremation grounds shall be situated; but that of the people of the highest caste shall be to the south (of the city).

Violation of this rule shall be punished with the first amercement.

Heretics and Chandálas shall live beyond the burial grounds.

Families of workmen may in any other way be provided with sites befitting with their occupation and field work. Besides working in flower-gardens, fruit-gardens, vegetable-gardens, and paddy-fields allotted to them, they (families) shall collect grains and merchandise in abundance as authorised.

There shall be a water-well for every ten houses.

Oils, grains, sugar, salt, medicinal articles, dry or fresh vegetables, meadow grass, dried flesh, haystock, firewood, metals, skins, charcoal, tendons (*snáyu*), poison, horns, bamboo, fibrous garments, strong timber, weapons, armour, and stones shall also be stored (in the fort) in such quantities as can be enjoyed for years together without feeling any want. Of such collection, old things shall be replaced by new ones when received.

Elephants, cavalry, chariots, and infantry shall each be officered with many chiefs inasmuch as chiefs, when many, are under the fear of betrayal from each other and scarcely liable to the insinuations and intrigues of an enemy.

The same rule shall hold good with the appointment of boundary, guards, and repairers of fortifications.

Never shall *báhirikas* who are dangerous to the well being of cities and countries be kept in forts. They may either be thrown in country parts or compelled to pay taxes.

V. THE DUTIES OF THE CHAMBERLAIN.

THE Chamberlain (*sannidhátá* = one who ever attends upon the king) shall see to the construction of the treasury-house, trading-house, the store-house of grains, the store-house of forest produce, the armoury and the jail.

Having dug up a square well not too deep to be moist with water, having paved both the bottom and the sides with slabs of stone, he shall, by using strong timber, construct in that well a cage-like under-ground chamber of three stories high, the top-most being on a level with the surface of the ground, with many compartments of various design, with floor plastered with small stones, with one door, with a movable staircase, and solemnised with the presence of the guardian deity.

Above this chamber, the treasury house closed on both sides, with projecting roofs and extensively opening into the store-house shall be built of bricks.

He may employ outcast men (*abhityakta-purusha*) to build at the extreme boundary of the kingdom a palacious mansion to hold substantial treasure against dangers and calamities.

The trading-house shall be a quadrangle enclosed by four buildings with one door, with pillars built of burnt bricks, with many compartments, and with a row of pillars on both sides kept apart.

The store-house shall consist of many spacious rooms and enclose within itself the store-house of forest produce separated from it by means of wall and connected with both the underground chamber and the armoury.

The court (*dharmasthíya*) and the office of the ministers (*mahámátríya*) shall be built in a separate locality.

Provided with separate accommodation for men and women kept apart and with many compartments well guarded, a jail shall also be constructed.

All these buildings shall be provided with halls (*sála*) pits (*kháta*—privy [?]), water-well, bath-room, remedies against fire and poison, with cats, mangooses, and with necessary means to worship the guardian gods appropriate to each.

In (front of) the store-house a bowl (*kunda*) with its mouth as wide as an *aratni* (24 *angulag*) shall be set up as rain-gauge (*varshamána*).

Assisted by experts having necessary qualifications and provided with tools and instruments, the chamberlain shall attend to the business of receiving gems either old or new, as well as raw materials of superior or inferior value.

In cases of deception in gems, both the deceiver and the abettor shall be punished with the highest amercement; in the case of superior commodities, they shall be punished with the middle-most amercement; and in that of commodities of inferior value, they shall be compelled not only to restore the same, but also pay a fine equal to the value of the articles.

He shall receive only such gold coins as have been declared to be pure by the examiner of coins.

Counterfeit coins shall be cut into pieces.

Whoever brings in counterfeit coins shall be punished with the first amercement.

Grains pure and fresh shall be received in full measures; otherwise a fine of twice the value of the grains shall be imposed.

The same rule shall hold good with the receipt of merchandise, raw materials, and weapons.

In all departments, whoever, whether as an officer (*yukta*), a clerk (*upayukta*), or a servant (*tatpurusha*), misappropriates sums from one to four panas or any other valuable things shall be punished with the first, middlemost, and highest amercements and death respectively.

If the officer who is in charge of the treasury causes loss in money, he shall be whipped (*ghátah*), while his abettors shall receive half the punishment; if the loss is due to ignorance, he shall be censured.

If, with the intention of giving a hint, robbers are frightened (by the guards), (the latter) shall be tortured to death.

Hence assisted by trustworthy persons, the chamberlain shall attend to the business of revenue collection.

He shall have so thorough a knowledge of both external and internal incomes running even for a hundred years that, when questioned, he can point out without hesitation the exact amount of net balance that remains after expenditure has been met with.

VI. THE BUSINESS OF COLLECTION OF REVENUE BY THE COLLECTOR-GENERAL.

THE Collector-General shall attend to (the collection of revenue from) forts (*durga*), country-parts (*ráshtra*), mines (*khani*), buildings and gardens (*setu*), forests (*vana*), herds of cattle (*vraja*), and roads of traffic (*vanikpatha*).

Tolls, fines, weights and measures, the town-clerk (*nágaraka*), the superintendent of coinage (*lakshanádhyakshah*), the superintendent of seals and pass-ports, liquor, slaughter of animals, threads, oils,. ghee, sugar (*kshára*), the state-goldsmith (*sauvarnika*), the warehouse of merchandise, the prostitute, gambling, building sites (*vástuka*), the corporation of artisans and handicrafts-men (*kárusilpiganah*), the superintendent of gods, and taxes collected at the gates and from the people (known as) *Báhirikas* come under the head of forts.

Produce from crown-lands (*sita*), portion of produce payable to the government (*bhága*), religious taxes (*bali*), taxes paid in money (*kara*), merchants, the superintendent of rivers, ferries, boats, and ships, towns, pasture grounds, road-cess (*vartani*), ropes (*rajjú*) and ropes to bind thieves (*chórarajjú*) come under the head of country parts.

Gold, silver, diamonds, gems, pearls, corals, conch-shells, metals (*loha*), salt, and other minerals extracted from plains and mountain slopes come under the head of mines.

Flower-gardens, fruit-gardens, vegetable-gardens, wet fields, and fields where crops are grown by sowing roots for seeds (*múlavápáh, i.e.*, sugar-cane crops, etc.) come under *sétu*.

Game-forests, timber-forests, and elephant-forests are forests.

Cows, buffaloes, goats, sheep, asses, camels, horses, and mules come under the head of herds.

Land and water ways are the roads of traffic.

All these form the body of income (*áyasaríram*).

Capital (*múla*), share (*bhága*), premia (*vyáji*), *parigha* (?) fixed taxes (*klripta*), premia on coins (*rúpika*), and fixed fines (*atyaya*) are the several forms of revenue (*áyamukha, i.e.*, the mouth from which income is to issue).

The chanting of auspicious hymns during the worship of gods and ancestors, and on the occasion of giving gifts, the harem, the kitchen, the establishment of messengers, the store-house, the armoury, the warehouse, the store-house of raw materials, manufactories (*karmánta*), free labourers (*vishti*), maintenance of infantry, cavalry, chariots, and elephants, herds of cows, the museum of beasts, deer, birds, and snakes, and storage of firewood and fodder constitute the body of expenditure (*vyayasaríram*).

The royal year, the month, the *paksha*, the day, the dawn (*vyushta*), the third and seventh *pakshas* of (the seasons such as) the rainy season, the winter season, and the summer short of their days, the rest complete, and a separate intercalary month are (the divisions of time).

He shall also pay attention to the work in hand (*karaníya*), the work accomplished (*siddham*), part of a work in hand (*sésha*), receipts, expenditure, and net balance.

The business of upkeeping the government (*samsthánam*), the routine work (*prachárah*), the collection of necessaries of life, the collection and audit of all kinds of revenue,—these constitute the work in hand.

That which has been credited to the treasury; that which has been taken by the king; that which has been spent in connection with the capital city not entered (into the register) or continued from year before last, the royal command dictated or orally intimated to be entered (into the register),—all these constitute the work accomplished.

Preparation of plans for profitable works, balance of fines due, demand for arrears of revenue kept in abeyance, and examination of accounts,—these constitute what is called part of a work in hand which may be of little or no value.

Receipts may be (1) current, (2) last balance, and (3) accidental (*anyajátah*= received from external source).

What is received day after day is termed current (*vartamána*).

Whatever has been brought forward from year before last, whatever is in the hands of others, and whatever has changed hands is termed last balance (*puryushita*).

Whatever has been lost and forgotten (by others), fines levied from government servants, marginal revenue (*pársva*), compensation levied for any damage (*párihínikam*), presentations to the king, the property of those who have fallen victims to epidemics (*damaragatakasvam*) leaving no sons, and treasure-troves,---all these constitute accidental receipts.

Investment of capital (*vikshépa*), the relics of a wrecked undertaking, and the savings from an estimated outlay are the means to check expenditure (*vyayapratyayah*).

The rise in price of merchandise due to the use of different weights and measures in selling is termed *vyáji*; the enhancement of price due to bidding among buyers is also another source of profit.

Expenditure is of two kinds—daily expenditure and profitable expenditure.

What is continued every day is daily.

Whatever is earned once in a *paksha*, a month, or a year is termed profit.

Whatever is spent on these two heads is termed as daily expenditure and profitable expenditure respectively.

That which remains after deducting all the expenditure already incurred and excluding all revenue to be realised is net balance (*nívi*) which may have been either just realised or brought forward.

Thus a wise collector-general shall conduct the work of revenue-collection, increasing the income and decreasing the expenditure.

VII. THE BUSINESS OF KEEPING UP ACCOUNTS IN THE OFFICE OF ACCOUNTANTS.

THE superintendent of accounts shall have the accountant's office constructed with its door facing either the north or the east, with seats (for clerks) kept apart and with shelves of account-books well arranged.

Therein the number of several departments; the description of the work carried on and of the results realised in several manufactories (*Karmánta*); the amount of profit, loss, expenditure, delayed earnings, the amount of *vyáji* (premia in kind or cash) realised,—the status of government agency employed, the amount of wages paid, the number of free labourers engaged (*vishti*) pertaining to the investment of capital on any work; likewise in the case of gems and commodities of superior or inferior value, the rate of their price, the rate of their barter, the counterweights (*pratimána*) used in weighing them, their number, their weight, and their cubical measure; the history of customs, professions, and transactions of countries, villages, families, and corporations; the gains in the form of gifts to the king's courtiers, their title to possess and enjoy lands, remission of taxes allowed to them, and payment of provisions and salaries to them; the gains to the wives and sons of the king in gems, lands, prerogatives, and provisions made to remedy evil portents; the treaties with, issues of ultimatum to, and payments of tribute from or to, friendly or inimical kings,— all these shall be regularly entered in prescribed registers.

From these books the superintendent shall furnish the accounts as to the forms of work in hand, of works accomplished, of part of works in hand, of receipts, of expenditure, of net balance, and of tasks to be undertaken in each of the several departments.

To supervise works of high, middling and low description, superintendents with corresponding qualifications shall be employed.

The king will have to suffer in the end if he curtails the fixed amount of expenditure on profitable works.

(When a man engaged by Government for any work absents himself), his sureties who conjointly received (wages?) from the government, or his sons, brothers, wives, daughters or servants living upon his work shall bear the loss caused to the Government.

The work of 354 days and nights is a year. Such a work shall be paid for more or less in proportion to its quantity at the end of the month, *Ashádha* (about the middle of July). (The work during) the intercalary month shall be (separately) calculated.

A government officer, not caring to know the information gathered by espionage and neglecting to supervise the despatch of work in his own department as regulated, may occasion loss of revenue to the government owing to his ignorance, or owing to his idleness when he is too weak to endure the trouble of activity, or due to inadvertence in perceiving sound and other objects of sense, or by being timid when he is afraid of clamour, unrighteousness, and untoward results, or owing to selfish desire when he is favourably disposed towards those who are desirous to achieve their own selfish ends, or by cruelty due to anger, or by lack of dignity when he is surrounded by a host of learned and needy sycophants, or by making use of false balance, false measures, and false calculation owing to greediness.

The school of Manu hold that a fine equal to the loss of revenue and multiplied by the serial number of the circumstances of the guilt just narrated in order shall be imposed upon him.

The school of *Parásara* hold that the fine in all the cases shall be eight times the amount lost.

The school of *Brihaspathi* say that it shall be ten times the amount.

The school of *Usanas* say that it shall be twenty times the amount.

But Kautilya says that it shall be proportional to the guilt.

Accounts shall be submitted in the month of *Ashádha*.

When they (the accountants of different districts) present themselves with sealed books, commodities and net revenue, they shall all be kept apart in one place so that they cannot carry on conversation with each other. Having heard from them the totals of receipts, expenditure, and net revenue, the net amount shall be received.

By how much the superintendent of a department augments the net total of its revenue either by increasing any one of the items of its receipts or by decreasing anyone of the items of expenditure, he shall be rewarded eight times that amount. But when it is reversed (*i.e.*, when the net total is decreased), the award shall also be reversed (*i.e.*, he shall be made to pay eight times the decrease).

Those accountants who do not present themselves in time or do not produce their account books along with the net revenue shall be fined ten times the amount due from them.

When a superintendent of accounts (*káranika*) does not at once proceed to receive and check the accounts when the clerks (*kármika*) are ready, he shall be punished with the first amercement. In the reverse case (*i.e.*, when the clerks are not ready), the clerks shall be punished with double the first amercement.

All the ministers (*mahámáras*) shall together narrate the whole of the actual accounts pertaining to each department.

Whoever of these (ministers or clerks ?) is of undivided counsel or keeps himself aloof, or utters falsehood shall be punished with the highest amercement.

When an accountant has not prepared the table of daily accounts (*akritáhorúpaharam*), he may be given a month more (for its preparation). After the lapse of one month he shall be fined at the rate of 200 *panas* for each month (during which he delays the accounts).

If an accountant has to write only a small portion of the accounts pertaining to net revenue, he may be allowed five nights to prepare it.

Then the table of daily accounts submitted by him along with the net revenue shall be checked with reference to the regulated forms of righteous transactions and precedents and by applying such arithmetical processes as addition, subtraction, inference and by espionage. It shall also be verified with reference to (such divisions of time as) days, five nights, *pakshás*, months, four-months, and the year.

The receipt shall be verified with reference to the place and time pertaining to them, the form of their collection (*i.e.*, capital, share), the amount of the present and past produce, the person who has paid it, the person who caused its payment, the officer who fixed the amount payable, and the officer who received it. The expenditure shall be verified with reference to the cause of the profit from any source in the place and time pertaining to each item, the amount payable, the amount paid, the person who ordered the collection, the person who remitted the same, the person who delivered it, and the person who finally received it.

Likewise the net revenue shall be verified with reference to the place, time, and source pertaining to it, its standard of fineness and quantity, and the persons who are employed to guard the deposits and magazines (of grains, etc.).

When an officer (*káranika*) does not facilitate or prevents the execution of the king's order, or renders the receipts and expenditure otherwise than prescribed, he shall be punished with the first amercement.

Any clerk who violates or deviates from the prescribed form of writing accounts, enters what is unknown to him, or makes double or treble entries (*punaruktam*) shall be fined 12 *panas*.

He who scrapes off the net total shall be doubly punished.

He who eats it up shall be fined eight times.

He who causes loss of revenue shall not only pay a fine equal to five times the amount lost (*panchabandha*), but also make good the loss. In case of uttering a lie, the punishment levied for theft shall be imposed. (When an entry lost or omitted) is made later or is made to appear as forgotten, but added later on recollection, the punishment shall be double the above.

The king shall forgive an offence when it is trifling, have satisfaction even when the revenue is scanty, and honour with rewards (*pragraha*) such of his superintendents as are of immense benefit to him.

VIII. DETECTION OF WHAT IS EMBEZZLED BY GOVERNMENT SERVANTS OUT OF STATE REVENUE.

ALL undertakings depend upon finance. Hence foremost attention shall be paid to the treasury.

Public prosperity (*prachárasamriddhih*), rewards for good conduct (*charitránugrahah*), capture of thieves, dispensing with (the service of too many) government servants, abundance of harvest, prosperity of commerce, absence of troubles and calamities (*upasargapramokshah*), diminution of remission of taxes, and income in gold (*hiranyópáyanam*) are all conducive to financial prosperity.

Obstruction (*pratibandha*), loan (*prayóga*), trading (*vyavahára*), fabrication of accounts (*avastára*), causing the loss of revenue (*parihápana*), self-enjoyment (*upabhóga*), barter (*parivartana*), and defalcation (*apahára*) are the causes that tend to deplete the treasury.

Failure to start an undertaking or to realise its results, or to credit its profits (to the treasury) is known as obstruction. Herein a fine of ten times the amount in question shall be imposed.

Lending the money of the treasury on periodical interest is a loan.

Carrying on trade by making use of government money is trading.

These two acts shall be punished with a fine of twice the profit earned.

Whoever makes as unripe the ripe time or as ripe the unripe time (of revenue collection) is guilty of fabrication. Herein a fine of ten times the amount (*panchabandha*) shall be imposed.

Whoever lessens a fixed amount of income or enhances the expenditure is guilty of causing the loss of revenue. Herein a fine of four times the loss shall be imposed.

Whoever enjoys himself or causes others to enjoy whatever belongs to the king is guilty of self-enjoyment. Herein death-sentence shall be passed for enjoying gems, middlemost amercement for enjoying valuable articles, and restoration of the articles together with a fine equal to their value shall be the punishment for enjoying articles of inferior value.

The act of exchanging government articles for (similar) articles of others is barter. This offence is explained by self-enjoyment.

Whoever does not take into the treasury the fixed amount of revenue collected, or does not spend what is ordered to be spent, or misrepresents the net revenue collected is guilty of defalcation of government money. Herein a fine of twelve times the amount shall be imposed.

There are about forty ways of embezzlement: what is realised earlier is entered later on; what is realised later is entered earlier; what ought to be realised is not realised; what is hard to realise is shown as realised; what is collected is shown as not collected; what has not been collected is shown as collected; what is collected in part is entered as collected in full; what is collected in full is entered as collected in part; what is collected is of one sort, while what is entered is of another sort; what is realised from one source is shown as realised from another; what is payable is not paid; what is not payable is paid; not paid in time; paid untimely; small gifts made large gifts; large gifts made small gifts; what is gifted is of one sort while what is entered is of another; the real donee is one while the person entered (in the register) as donee is another; what has been taken into (the treasury) is removed while what has not been credited to it is shown as credited; raw materials that are not paid for are entered, while those that are paid for are not entered; an aggregate is scattered in pieces; scattered items are converted into an aggregate; commodities of greater value are bartered for those of small value; what is of smaller value is bartered for one of greater value; price of commodities enhanced; price of commodities lowered; number of nights increased; number of nights decreased; the year not in harmony with its months; the month not in harmony with its days; inconsistency in the transactions carried on with personal supervision (*samágamavishánah*); misrepresentation of the source of income; inconsistency in giving charities; incongruity in representing the work turned out; inconsistency in dealing with fixed items; misrepresentation of test marks or the standard of fineness (of gold and silver); misrepresentation of prices of commodities; making use of false weight and measures; deception in counting articles; and making use of false cubic measures such as *bhájan*— these are the several ways of embezzlement.

Under the above circumstances, the persons concerned such as the treasurer (*nidháyaka*), the prescriber (*nibandhaka*), the receiver (*pratigráhaka*), the payer (*dáyaka*), the person who caused the payment (dápaka), the ministerial servants of the officer (*mantri-vaiyávrityakara*) shall each be separately examined. If any one of these tells a lie, he shall receive the same punishment as the chief-officer, (*yukta*) who committed the offence.

A proclamation in public (*prachára*) shall be made to the effect "whoever has suffered at the hands of this offender may make their grievances known to the king."

Those who respond to the call shall receive such compensation as is equal to the loss they have sustained.

When there are a number of offences in which a single officer is involved, and when his being guilty of *parókta* in any one of those charges has been established, he shall be answerable for all those offences. Otherwise (*i.e.,* when it is not established), he shall be tried for each of the charges.

When a government servant has been proved to be guilty of having misappropriated part of a large sum in question, he shall be answerable for the whole.

Any informant (*súchaka*) who supplies information about embezzlement just under perpetration shall, if he succeeds in proving it, get as reward one-sixth of the amount in question; if he happens to be a government servant (*bhritaka*), he shall get for the same act one-twelfth of the amount.

If an informant succeeds in proving only a part of a big embezzlement, he shall, nevertheless, get the prescribed share of the part of the embezzled amount proved.

An informant who fails to prove (his assertion) shall be liable to monetary or corporal punishment, and shall never be acquitted.

When the charge is proved, the informant may impute the tale-bearing to someone else or clear himself in any other way from the blame. Any informant who withdraws his assertion prevailed upon by the insinuations of the accused shall be condemned to death.

IX. EXAMINATION OF THE CONDUCT OF GOVERNMENT SERVANTS.

THOSE who are possessed of ministerial qualifications shall, in accordance with their individual capacity, be appointed as superintendents of government departments. While engaged in work, they shall be daily examined; for men are naturally fickle-minded and like horses at work exhibit constant change in their temper. Hence the agency and tools which they make use of, the place and time of the work they are engaged in, as well as the precise form of the work, the outlay, and the results shall always be ascertained.

Without dissension and without any concert among themselves, they shall carry on their work as ordered.

When in concert, they eat up (the revenue).

When in disunion, they mar the work.

Without bringing to the knowledge of their master (*bhartri*, the king), they shall undertake nothing except remedial measures against imminent dangers.

A fine of twice the amount of their daily pay and of the expenditure (incurred by them) shall be fixed for any inadvertence on their part.

Whoever of the superintendents makes as much as, or more than, the amount of fixed revenue shall be honoured with promotion and rewards.

(My) teacher holds that that officer who spends too much and brings in little revenue eats it up; while he who proves the revenue (*i.e.*, brings in more than he spends) as well as the officer who brings inasmuch as he spends does not eat up the revenue.

But Kautilya holds that cases of embezzlement or no embezzlement can be ascertained through spies alone.

Whoever lessens the revenue eats the king's wealth. If owing to inadvertence he causes diminution in revenue, he shall be compelled to make good the loss.

Whoever doubles the revenue eats into the vitality of the country. If he brings in double the amount to the king, he shall, if the offence is small, be warned not to repeat the same; but if the offence be grave he should proportionally be punished.

Whoever spends the revenue (without bringing in any profit) eats up the labour of workmen. Such an officer shall be punished in proportion to the value of the work done, the number of days taken, the amount of capital spent, and the amount of daily wages paid.

Hence the chief officer of each department (*adhikarana*) shall thoroughly scrutinise the real amount of the work done, the receipts realised from, and the expenditure incurred in that departmental work both in detail and in the aggregate.

He shall also check (*pratishedhayet*) prodigal, spend-thrift and niggardly persons.

Whoever unjustly eats up the property left by his father and grandfather is a prodigal person (*múlahara*).

Whoever eats all that he earns is a spendthrift (*tádátvika*).

Whoever hordes money, entailing hardship both on himself and his servants is niggardly.

Whoever of these three kinds of persons has the support of a strong party shall not be disturbed; but he who has no such support shall be caught hold of (*paryádátavyah*).

Whoever is niggardly in spite of his immense property, hordes, deposits, or sends out—hordes in his own house, deposits with citizens or country people or sends out to foreign countries;—a spy shall find out the advisers, friends, servants, relations, partisans, as well as the income and expenditure of such a niggardly person. Whoever in a foreign country carries out the work of such a niggardly person shall be prevailed upon to give out the secret. When the secret is known, the niggardly person shall be murdered apparently under the orders of (his) avowed enemy.

Hence the superintendents of all the departments shall carry on their respective works in company with accountants, writers, coin-examiners, the treasurers, and military officers (*uttarádhyaksha*).

Those who attend upon military officers and are noted for their honesty and good conduct shall be spies to watch the conduct of accountants and other clerks.

Each department shall be officered by several temporary heads.

Just as it is impossible not to taste the honey or the poison that finds itself at the tip of the tongue, so it is impossible for a government servant not to eat up, at least, a bit of the king's revenue. Just as fish moving under water cannot possibly be found out either as drinking or not drinking water, so government servants employed in the government work cannot be found out (while) taking money (for themselves).

It is possible to mark the movements of birds flying high up in the sky; but not so is it possible to ascertain the movement of government servants of hidden purpose.

Government servants shall not only be confiscated of their ill-earned hordes, but also be transferred from one work to another, so that they cannot either misappropriate Government money or vomit what they have eaten up.

Those who increase the king's revenue instead of eating it up and are loyally devoted to him shall be made permanent in service.

X. THE PROCEDURE OF FORMING ROYAL WRITS.

(TEACHERS) say that (the word) *sásana*, command, (is applicable only to) royal writs (*sásana*).

Writs are of great importance to kings inasmuch as treaties and ultimate leading to war depend upon writs.

Hence one who is possessed of ministerial qualifications, acquainted with all kinds of customs, smart in composition, good in legible writing, and sharp in reading shall be appointed as a writer (*lékhaka*).

Such a writer, having attentively listened to the king's order and having well thought out the matter under consideration, shall reduce the order to writing.

As to a writ addressed to a lord (*ísvara*), it shall contain a polite mention of his country, his possessions, his family and his name, and as to that addressed to a common man (*anisvara*), it shall make a polite mention of his country and name.

Having paid sufficient attention to the caste, family, social rank, age, learning (*sruta*), occupation, property, character (*síla*), blood-relationship (*yaunánubandha*) of the addressee, as well as to the place and time (of writing), the writer shall form a writ befitting the position of the person addressed.

Arrangement of subject-matter (*arthakrama*), relevancy (*sambandha*), completeness, sweetness, dignity, and lucidity are the necessary qualities of a writ.

The act of mentioning facts in the order of their importance is arrangement.

When subsequent facts are not contradictory to facts just or previously mentioned, and so on till the completion of the letter, it is termed relevancy.

Avoidance of redundancy or deficiency in words or letters; impressive description of subject matter by citing reasons, examples, and illustrations; and the use of appropriate and suitably strong words (*asrántapada*) is completeness.

The description in exquisite style of a good purport with a pleasing effect is sweetness.

The use of words other than colloquial (*agrámya*) is dignity.

The use of well-known words is lucidity.

The alphabetical letters beginning with *Akára* are sixty-three.

The combination of letters is a word (*pada*). The word is of four kinds—nouns, verbs, prefixes of verbs, and particles (*nipáta*).

A noun is that which signifies an essence (*satva*).

A verb is that which has no definite gender and signifies an action.

'*Pra*' and other words are the prefixes of verbs.

'*Cha*' and other indeclinable words are particles.

A group of words conveying a complete sense is a sentence (*vákya*).

Combination of words (*varga*) consisting of not more than three words and not less than one word shall be so formed as to harmonise with the meaning of immediately following words.

The word, *'iti,'* is used to indicate the completion of a writ; and also to indicate an oral message as in the phrase *'váchikamasyeti,'* an oral message along with this (writ).

Calumniation (*nindá*), commendation, inquiry, narration request, refusal, censure, prohibition, command, conciliation, promise of help, threat, and persuasion are the thirteen purposes for which writs are issued.

Calumniation (*nindá*) consists in speaking ill of one's family, body and acts.

Commendation (*prasamsá*) consists in praising one's family, person, and acts.

To inquire 'how is this?' is inquiry.

To point out the way as 'thus,' is narration (*ákhyána*).

To entreat as '*give*,' is request.

To say that 'I do not give,' is refusal.

To say that 'it is not worthy of thee,' is censure (*upálambhah*).

To say as 'do not do so,' is prohibition (*pratishedha*).

To say that 'this should be done,' is command (*chódaná*).

To say 'what I am, thou art that; whichever article is mine is thine also, is conciliation (*sántvam*).

To hold out help in trouble is promise of help (*abhyavapattih*).

Pointing out the evil consequences that may occur in future is threat (*abhibartsanam*).

Persuasion is of three kinds: that made for the purpose of money, that made in case of one's failure to fulfill a promise, and that made on occasion of any trouble.

Also writs of information, of command, and of gift; likewise writs of remission, of licence, of guidance, of reply, and of general proclamation are other varieties.

Thus says (the messenger); so says (the king); if there is any truth in this (statement of the messenger), then the thing (agreed to) should at once be surrendered; (the messenger) has informed the king of all the deeds of the enemy. (*Parakára*);—this is the writ of information which is held to be of various forms.

Wherever and especially regarding Government servants the king's order either for punishment or for rewards is issued, it is called writ of command (*ájnálékha*).

Where the bestowal of honour for deserving merit is contemplated either as help to alleviate affliction (*ádhi*) or as gift (*paridána*), there are issued writs of gift (*upagrahalekha*).

Whatever favour (*anugraha*) to special castes, cities, villages, or countries of various description is announced in obedience to the king's order, it is called writ of remission (*pariháralékha*) by those who know it.

Likewise licence or permission (*nisrishti*) shall be enjoined either in word or deed; accordingly it is styled verbal order or writ of licence.

Various kinds of providential visitations or well ascertained evils of human make are believed to be the cause for issuing writs of guidance (*pravrittilékha*) to attempt remedies against them.

When having read a letter and discussed as to the form of reply thereto, a reply in accordance with the king's order is made, it is called a writ of reply (*pratilékha*).

When the king directs his viceroys (*isvara*) and other officers to protect and give material help to travellers either on roads or in the interior of the country, it is termed writ of general proclamation (*sarvatraga lekha*)

Negotiation, bribery, causing dissension, and open attack are forms of stratagem (*upáya*).

Negotiation is of five kinds:—

Praising the qualities (of an enemy), narrating the mutual relationship, pointing out mutual benefit, showing vast future prospects, and identity of interests.

When the family, person, occupation, conduct, learning, properties, etc. (of an enemy) are commended with due attention to their worth, it is termed praising the qualities (*gunasankírthana*).

When the fact of having agnates, blood-relations, teachers (*maukha*), priestly heirarchy (*srauva*), family, and friends in common is pointed out, it is known as narration of mutual relationship (*sambandhópakhyána*).

When both parties, the party of a king and that of his enemy are shown to be helpful to each other, it is known as pointing out mutual benefit (*parasparópakárasamdarsanam*).

Inducement such as 'this being done thus, such result will accrue to both of us,' is showing vast future prospects (*Ayátipradarsanam*).

To say 'what I am, that thou art; thou mayest utilize in thy works whatever is mine,' is identity of interests (*átmópanidhánam*).

Offering money is bribery (*upapradána*).

Causing fears and suspicion as well as threatening is known as sowing dissension.

Killing, harassing, and plundering is attack (*danda*).

Clumsiness, contradiction, repetition, bad grammar, and misarrangement are the faults of a writ.

Black and ugly leaf, (*kálapatrakamacháru*) and uneven and uncoloured (*virága*) writing cause clumsiness (*akánti*).

Subsequent portion disagreeing with previous portion of a letter, causes contradiction (*vyágháta*).

Stating for a second time what has already been said above is repetition.

Wrong use of words in gender, number, time and case is bad grammar (*apasabda*).

Division of paragraphs (*varga*) in unsuitable places, omission of necessary division of paragraphs, and violation of any other necessary qualities of a writ constitute misarrangement (*samplava*).

Having followed all sciences and having fully observed forms of writing in vogue, these rules of writing royal writs have been laid down by Kautilya in the interest of kings.

XI. EXAMINATION OF GEMS THAT ARE TO BE ENTERED INTO THE TREASURY.

THE Superintendent of the treasury shall, in the presence of qualified persons, admit into the treasury whatever he ought to, gems (*ratna*) and articles of superior or inferior value.

Támraparnika, that which is produced in the *támraparni*; *Pándyakavátaka,* that which is obtained in *Pándyakavata*; *Pásikya,* that which is produced in the *Pása*; *Kauleya,* that which is produced in the *kúla*; *Chaurneya,* that which is produced in the *Chúrna*; *Mahéndra,* that which is obtained near the mountain of *Mahéndra*; *Kárdamika,* that which is produced in the *Kárdama*; *Srautasíya,* that which is produced in the *Sròtasi*; *Hrádíya,* that which is produced in (a deep pool of water known as) *Hrada*; and *Haimavata,* that which is obtained in the vicinity of the Himalayas are the several varieties of pearls.

Oyster-shells, conch-shells, and other miscellaneous things are the wombs of pearls.

That which is like *masúra* (*ervum hirsutam*), that which consists of three joints (*triputaka*), that which is like a tortoise (*kúrmaka*), that which is semi-circular, that which consists of several coatings, that which is double (*yámaka*), that which is scratched, that which is of rough surface, that which is possessed of spots (*siktakam*), that which is like the water-pot used by an ascetic, that which is of dark-brown or blue colour, and that which is badly perforated are inauspicious.

That which is big, circular, without bottom (*nistalam*), brilliant, white, heavy, soft to the touch, and properly perforated is the best.

Sirshaka, upasirshaka, prakándaka, avaghátaka, and *taralapratibandha* are several varieties of pearl necklaces.

One thousand and eight strings of pearls form the necklace, *Indrachchhanda.*

Half of the above is *Vijayachchhanda.*

Sixty-four strings make up *Ardhahára.*

Fifty-four strings make up *Rasmikalápa.*

Thirty-two strings make up *Guchchha*.

Twenty-seven strings make up *Nakshatramála*.

Twenty-four strings make up *Ardhaguchchha*.

Twenty strings make up *Mánavaka*.

Half of the above is *Ardhamánavaka*.

The same necklaces with a gem at the centre are called by the same names with the words '*Mánavaka*' suffixed to their respective names.

When all the strings making up a necklace are of *sirshaka* pattern, it is called pure necklace (*suddhahára*); likewise with strings of other pattern. That which contains a gem in the centre is (also) called *Ardhamánavaka*.

That which contains three slab-like gems (*triphalaka*) or five slab-like gems (*panchaphalaka*) in the centre is termed *Phalakahára*.

An only string of pearls is called pure *Ekávali*; the same with a gem in the centre is called *Yashti*; the same variegated with gold globules is termed *Ratnávali*.

A string made of pearls and gold globules alternately put is called *Apavartaka*.

Strings of pearls with a gold wire between two strings is called *Sopánaka*.

The same with a gem in the centre is called *Manisópánaka*.

The above will explain the formation of head-strings, bracelets, anklets, waist-bands, and other varieties.

Kauta, that which is obtained in the *Kúta*; *Mauleyaka*, that which is found in the *Múleya*; and *Párasamudraka*, that which is found beyond the ocean are several varieties of gems.

That which possesses such pleasant colour as that of the red lotus flower, or that of the flower of *Párijáta* (*Erithrina Indica*), or that of the rising sun is the *Saugandhika* gem.

That which is of the colour of blue lotus flower, or of *sirísha* (*Acacia Sirisa*), or of water, or of fresh bamboo, or of the colour of the feathers of a parrot is the *Vaidúrya* gem *Pushyarága*, *Gómútraka*, and *Gómédika* are other varieties of the same.

That which is characterised with blue lines, that which is of the colour of the flower of *Kaláya* (a kind of *phraseolus*), or which is intensely blue, which possesses the colour of *Jambu* fruit (rose apple), or which is as blue as the clouds is the*Indraníla* gem; *Nandaka* (pleasing gem), *Sravanmadhya* (that which appears to pour water from its centre), *Sítavrishti* (that which appears to pour cold shower), and *Súryakánta* (sunstone) are other forms of gems.

Gems are hexagonal, quadrangular, or circular possessed of dazzling glow, pure, smooth, heavy, brilliant, transparent (*antargataprabha*) and illuminating; such are the qualities of gems.

Faint colour, sandy layer, spots, holes, bad perforation, and scratches are the defects of gems.

Vimalaka (pure), *sasyaka* (plant-like), *Anjanamúlaka* (deep-dark), *Pittaka* (like the bile of a cow) *Sulabhaka* (easily procurable), *Lohitaka* (red), *Amritámsuka* (of white rays), *Jyótírasaka* (glowing), *Maileyaka*, *Ahichchhatraka* , (procured in the country of *Ahichchhatra*), *Kúrpa*, *Pútikúrpa*, and *Sugandhikúrpa*, *Kshírapaka*, *Suktichúrnaka* (like the powder of an oystershell), *Silápraválaka* (like coral), *Pulaka*, *Súkrapulaka* are varieties of inferior gems.

The rest are metalic beads (*káchamani*).

Sabháráshtraka, that which is found in the country of *Sabháráshtra*; *Madhyamaráshtraka*, that which is found in the Central Province; *Kásmaka*, that which is found in the country of *Kásmaka*; *Sríkatanaka*, that which is found in the vicinity of the mountain, *Vedótkata*; *Manimantaka*, that which is found near the mountain *Maniman* or *Manimanta*; and *Indravánaká* are diamonds.

Mines, streams, and other miscellaneous places are their sources.

The colour of a diamond may be like that of a cat's eye, that of the flower of *Sirísha* (*Acacia Sirísa*), the urine of a cow, the bile of a cow, like alum (*sphatika*), the flower of *Málati*, or like that of any of the gems (described above).

That which is big, heavy, hard (*prahárasaham*, tolerant of hitting), regular (*samakóna*), capable of scratching on the surface of vessels (*bhájanalékhi*), refractive of light (*kubrámi*), and brilliant is the best.

That which is devoid of angles, uneven (*nirasríkam*), and bent on one side (*pársvápavrittam*) is inauspicious.

Alakandaka, and *Vaivarnaka* are the two varieties of coral which is possessed of ruby-like colour, which is very hard, and which is free from the contamination of other substances inside.

Sátana is red and smells like the earth; *Gósirshaka* is dark red and smells like fish; *Harichandana* is of the colour of the feathers of a parrot and smells like tamarind or mango fruit; likewise *Tárnasa*; *Grámeruka* is red or dark red and smells like the urine of a goat; *Daivasabheya* is red and smells like a lotus flower; likewise *Aupaka* (*Jápaka*); *Jongaka* and *Taurupa* are red or dark red and soft; *Maleyaka* is reddish white; *Kuchandana* is as black as *Agaru* (resin of the aloe) or red or dark red and very rough; *Kála-parvataka* is of pleasant appearance; *Kosákaraparvataka* (that which is the product of that mountain which is of the shape of a bud) is black or variegated black; *Sítódakíya* is black and soft, and smells like a lotus-flower; *Nágaparvataka* (that which is the product of Naga mountain) is rough and is possessed of the colour of *Saivala* (*Vallisneria*); and *Sákala* is brown.

Light, soft, moist (*asyána*, not dry), as greasy as ghee, of pleasant smell, adhesive to the skin, of mild smell, retentive of colour and smell, tolerant of heat, absorptive of heat, and comfortable to the skin--these are the characteristics of sandal (*chandana*).

(As to) *Agaru* (*Agallochum*, resin of aloe):—

Jongaka is black or variegated black and is possessed of variegated spots; *Dongaka* is black; and *Párasamudraka* is of variegated colour and smells like cascus or like *Navamálika* (*jasminum*).

(*Agaru* is) heavy, soft, greasy, smells far and long, burns slowly, gives out continuous smoke while burning, is of uniform smell, absorbs heat, and is so adhesive to the skin as not to be removable by rubbing;—these are the characteristics of *Agaru*.

(As to) *Tailaparnika*:—

Asókagrámika, the product of *Asókagráma*, is of the colour of meat and smells like a lotus flower; *Jongaka* is reddish yellow and smells like a blue lotus flower or like the urine of a cow; *Grameruka* is greasy and smells like a cow's urine;*Sauvarnakudyaka*, product of the country of *Suvarnakudya*, is reddish yellow and smells like *Mátulunga* (the fruit of citron tree or sweet lime); *Púrnadvipaka*, the product of the island, *Púrnadviipa*, smells like a lotus flower or like butter;*Bhadrasríya* and *Páralauhityaka* are of the colour of nutmeg; *Antarvatya* is of the colour of cascus,---the last two smell like *Kushtha* (*Costus Speciosus*); *Kaleyaka* which is a product of *Svarna-bhúmi*, gold-producing land, is yellow and greasy; and *Auttaraparvataka* (a product of, the north mountain) is reddish yellow.

The above (fragrant substances) are commodities of superior value (*Sára*). The smell of the *Tailaparnika* substances is lasting, no matter whether they are made into a paste or boiled or burnt; also it is neither changed nor affected even when mixed with other substances; and these substances resemble sandal and*Agallochum* in their qualities.

Kántanávaka, *Praiyaka*, and *Auttara-parvataka* are the varieties of skins.*Kántanávaka* is of the colour of the neck of the peacock; *Praiyaka* is variegated with blue, yellow, and white spots; these two are eight *angulas* (inches) long.

Also *Bisí* and *Mahábisí* are the products of *Dvádasagráma*, twelve villages.

That which is of indistinct colour, hairy, and variegated (with spots) is (called) *Bisí*.

That which is rough and almost white is *Mahábisí* (great *Bisí*); These two are twelve angulas long.

Syámika, Kálika, Kadali, Chandrottara, and *Sákulá* are (other kinds of skins) procured from *Aroha* (*Arohaja*).

Syámika is brown and contains variegated spots; *Kálika* is brown or of the colour of a pigeon; these two are eight angulas long. *Kadali* is rough and two feet long; when *Kadali* bears variegated moonlike spots, it is called*Chandrottarakadali* and is one-third of its length; *Sákulá* is variegated with large round spots similar to those that manifest themselves in a kind of leprosy (*kushtha*), or is furnished with tendrils and spotted like a deer's skin.

Sámúra, Chínasi, and *Sámúli* are (skins procured from *Báhlava*, (*Bahlaveya*).

Sámúra is thirty-six angulas long and black; *Chínasi* is reddish black or blackish white; *Sámúli* is of the colour of wheat.

Sátina, Nalatúla, and *Vrittapuchchha* are the skins of aquatic animals (*Audra*).

Sátina is black; *Nalatúla* is of the colour of the fibre of *Nala*, a kind of grass; and *Vrittapuchchha* (that which possesses a round tail) is brown.

The above are the varieties of skins. Of skins, that which is soft, smooth and hairy is the best. Blankets made of sheep's wool may be white, purely red, or as red as a lotus flower. They may be made of worsted threads by sewing (*khachita*); or may be woven of woollen threads of various colour (*vánachitra*); or may be made of different pieces (*khandasanghátya*); or may be woven of uniform woollen threads (*tantuvichchhinna*).

Woollen blankets are (of ten kinds):—*Kambala, Kauchapaka, Kulamitika, Saumitika, Turagastarana, Varna ka, Talichchhaka, Váraváná, Paristoma*, and *Samantabhadraka*.

Of these, that which is slippery (*pichchhila*) as a wet surface, possessed of fine hair, and soft, is the best.

That (blanket) which is made up of eight pieces and black in colour is called *Bhingisi* used as rain-proof ; likewise is *Apasáraka*; both are the products of Nepal.

Samputika, *Chaturasrika*, *Lambara*, *Katavánaka*, *Praváraka*, and *Sattalika* are (blankets made of) the wool of wild animals.

That which is manufactured in the country, *Vanga* (*vangaka*) is a white and soft fabric (*dukúla*); that of *Pándya* manufacture (*Paundraka*) is black and as soft as the surface of a gem; and that which is the product of the country,*Suvarnakudya*, is as red as the sun, as soft as the surface of the gem, woven while the threads are very wet, and of uniform (*chaturasra*) or mixed texture (*vyámisravána*).

Single, half, double, treble and quadruple garments are varieties of the same.The above will explain other kinds of fabrics such as *Kásika*, *Benarese* products, and *Kshauma* which is manufactured in *Pándya* (*Paundraka*). *Mágadhika* (product of the *Magadha* countr y), *Paundraka*, and *Sauvarnakudyaka* are fibrous garments.

Nágavriksha (a species of a tree), *Likucha* (*Artocarpus Lakucha*), and *Vakula* (*Mimusops Elengi*), and *Vata* (*Ficus Indica*) are the sources (of their fibres).

That of *Nágavriksha* is yellow (*pita*); that of *Likucha* is of the colour of wheat; that of *Vakula* is white; and the rest is of the colour of butter.Of these, that which is produced in the country of *Suvarnakudya* is the best.

The above will explain the fabrics known as *kauseya*, silk-cloth, and *chinapatta*, fabrics of China manufacture.Of cotton fabrics, those of *Madhura*, of *Aparánta*, western parts, of *Kálinga*, of *Kási*, of *Vanga*, of *Vatsa*, and of *Mahisha* are the best.

As to other kinds of gems (which are not treated of here), the superintendent shall ascertain their size, their value, species, form, utility, their treatment, the repair of old ones, any adulteration that is not easily detected, their wear and tear due to lapse of time and place, as well as remedies against those which are inauspicious (*himsra*).

XII. CONDUCTING MINING OPERATIONS AND MANUFACTURE.

POSSESSED of the knowledge of the science dealing with copper and other minerals (*Sulbádhátusástra*), experienced in the art of distillation and condensation of mercury (*rasapáka*) and of testing gems, aided by experts in mineralogy and equipped with mining labourers and necessary instruments, the superintendent of mines shall examine mines which, on account of their containing mineral excrement (*kitta*), crucibles, charcoal, and ashes, may appear to have been once exploited or which may be newly discovered on plains or mountain-slopes possessing mineral ores, the richness of which can be ascertained by weight, depth of colour, piercing smell, and taste.

Liquids which ooze out from pits, eaves, slopes, or deep excavations of well-known mountains; which have the colour of the fruit of rose-apple (*jambu*), of mango, and of *fanpalm*; which are as yellow as ripe turmeric, sulphurate of arsenic (*haritála*), honey-comb, and vermilion; which are as resplendent as the petals of a lotus, or the feathers of a parrot or a peacock; which are adjacent to (any mass of) water or shrubs of similar colour; and which are greasy (*chikkana*), transparent (*visada*), and very heavy are ores of gold (*kánchanika*). Likewise liquids which, when dropped on water, spread like oil to which dirt and filth adhere, and which amalgamate themselves more than cent per cent (*satádupari veddhárah*) with copper or silver.

Of similar appearance as the above (*tatpratirúpakam*), but of piercing smell and taste is Bitumen.

Those ores which are obtained from plains or slopes of mountains; which are either yellow or as red as copper or reddish yellow; which are disjoined and marked with blue lines; which have the colour of black beans (*masha, PhraseolusRadiatus*), green beans (*mudga, Phraseolus Mungo*), and sesamum; which are marked with spots like a drop of curd and resplendent as turmeric, yellow myrobalan, petals of a lotus, acquatic plant, the liver or the spleen; which possess a sandy layer within them and are marked with figures of a circle or a *svastika*; which contain globular masses (*sagulika*); and which, when roasted do not split, but emit much foam and smoke are the ores of gold (*suvarnadhátavah*), and are used to form amalgams with copper or silver (*pratívápárthasté stámrarúpyavedharáh*).

Those ores which have the colour of a conch-shell, camphor, alum, butter, a pigeon, turtle-dove, *Vimalaka* (a kind of precious stone), or the neck of a peacock; which are as resplendent as opal (*sasyaka*), agate (*gomédaka*), cane-sugar (*guda*), and granulated sugar (*matsyandika*) which has the colour of the flower of *kovidára* (*Bauhinia Variegata*), of lotus, of *patali* (*Bignonia Suaveolens*), of *kalaya* (a kind of *phraseolus*), of *kshauma* (flax), and of *atasi* (*DinuinUsitatissimum*); which may be in combination with lead or iron (*anjana*); which smell like raw meat, are disjoined gray or blackish white, and are marked with lines or spots; and which, when roasted, do not split, but emit much foam and smoke are silver ores.

The heavier the ores, the greater will be the quantity of metal in them (*satvavriddhih*).

The impurities of ores, whether superficial or inseparably combined with them can be got rid of and the metal melted when the ores are (chemically) treated with Tikshna urine (*mútra*) and alkalies (*kshára*), and are mixed or smeared over with the mixture of (the powder of) *Rajavriksha* (*Clitoria Ternatea*), *Vata* (*Ficus Indica*), and *Pelu* (*Carnea Arborea*), together with cow's bile and the urine and dung of a buffalo, an ass and an elephant.

(Metals) are rendered soft when they are treated with (the powder of) *kandali* (mushroom), and *vajrakanda*, (Antiquorum) together with the ashes of barley, black beans, *palása* (*Butea Frondosa*), and *pelu* (*Carnea Arborea*), or with the milk of both the cow and the sheep. Whatever metal is split into a hundred thousand parts is rendered soft when it is thrice soaked in the mixture made up of honey (*madhu*), *madhuka* (*Bassia Latifolia*), sheep's milk, sesamum oil, clarified butter, jaggery, *kinva* (ferment) and mushroom.

Permanent softness (*mridustambhana*) is also attained when the metal is treated with the powder of cow's teeth and horn.

Those ores which are obtained from plains or slopes of mountains; and which are heavy, greasy, soft, tawny, green, dark, bluish-yellow (*harita*), pale-red, or red are ores of copper.

Those ores which have the colour of *kákamechaka* (*Solanum Indica*), pigeon, or cow's bile, and which are marked with white lines and smell like raw meat are the ores of lead.

Those ores which are as variegated in colour as saline soil or which have the colour of a burnt lump of earth are the ores of tin.

Those ores which are of orange colour (*kurumba*), or pale-red (*pándurohita*), or of the colour of the flower of *sinduvára* (*Vitex Trifolia*) are the ores of *tíkshna*. Those ores which are of the colour of the leaf of *kánda* (*Artemisia Indica*) or of the leaf of birch are the ores of *vaikrintaka*.

Pure, smooth, effulgent, sounding (when struck), very hard (*satatívrah*), and of little colour (*tanurága*) are precious stones.

The yield of mines may be put to such uses as are in vogue.

Commerce in commodities manufactured from mineral products shall be centralized and punishment for manufacturers, sellers, and purchasers of such commodities outside the prescribed locality shall also be laid down.

A mine-labourer who steals mineral products except precious stones shall be punished with a fine of eight times their value.

Any person who steals mineral products or carries on mining operations without license shall be bound (with chains) and caused to work (as a prisoner).

Mines which yield such minerals as are made use of in preparing vessels (*bhánda*) as well as those mines which require large outlay to work out may be leased out for a fixed number of the shares of the output or for a fixed rent (*bhágenaprakrayena va*) Such mines as can be worked out without much outlay shall be directly exploited (by Government agency).

The superintendent of metals (*lóhádhyakshah*) shall carry on the manufacture of copper, lead, tin, *vaikrintaka* (mercury [?]), *árakúta* (brass), *vritta*(?); *kamsa* (bronze or bell-metal), *tála* (sulphurate of arsenic), and *lodhra* (?), and also of commodities (*bhánda*) from them.

The superintendent of mint (*lakshnádhyakshah*), shall carry on the manufacture of silver coins (*rúpyarúpa*) made up of four parts of copper and one-sixteenth part (*másha*) of any one of the metals, *tikshna*, *trapu*, *sisa*, and *anjana*. There shall be a *pana*, half a *pana*, a quarter and one-eighth.

Copper coins (*támrarúpa*) made up of four parts of an alloy (*pádajívam*), shall be a *máshaka*, half a *máshaka*, *kákani* and half a *kákani*.

The examiner of coins (*rúpadarsaka*) shall regulate currency both as a medium of exchange (*vyávahárikim*) and as legal tender admissible into the treasury (*kosapravesyám*): The premia levied on coins paid into the treasury shall be) 8 per cent, known as *rúpika*, 5 per cent known as *vyáji*, one-eighth *pana* per cent as *páríkshika* (testing charge), besides (cha) a fine of 25 *pana* to be imposed on offenders other than the manufacturer, the seller, the purchaser and the examiner.

The superintendent of ocean-mines (*khanyadhyakshah*) shall attend to the collection of conch-shells, diamonds, precious stones, pearls, corals, and salt (*kshára*) and also regulate the commerce in the above commodities.

Soon after crystalisation of salt is over, the superintendent of salt shall in time collect both the money-rent (*prakraya*) and the quantity of the shares of salt due to the government; and by the sale of salt (thus collected as shares) he shall realise not only its value (*múlyam*), but also the premium of five per cent (*vyájím*), both in cash (*rúpa*).

Imported salt (*ágantulavanam*) shall pay one-sixth portion (*shadbhága*) to the king. The sale of this portion (*bhágavibhága*) shall fetch the premia of five per cent (*vyáji*), of eight per cent (*rúpika*) in cash (*rúpa*). The purchasers shall pay not only the toll (*sulka*), but also the compensation (*vaidharana*) equivalent to the loss entailed on the king's commerce. In default of the above payment, he shall be compelled to pay a fine of 600 *panas*.

Adulteration of salt shall be punished with the highest amercement; likewise persons other than hermits (*vánaprastha*) manufacturing salt without license.

Men learned in the Vedas, persons engaged in penance, as well as labourers may take with them salt for food; salt and alkalies for purposes other than this shall be subject to the payment of toll.

Thus; besides collecting from mines the ten kinds of revenue, such as (1) value of the out-put (*múlya*), (2) the share of the out-put (*vibhága*), (3) the premium of five per cent (*vyáji*), (4) the testing charge of coins (*parigha*), (5) fine previously announced (*atyaya*), (6) toll (*sulka*), (7) compensation for loss entailed on the king's commerce (*vaidharana*), (8) fines to be determined in proportion to the gravity of crimes (*danda*), (9), coinage (*rúpa*), (10) the premium of eight per cent (*rúpika*), the government shall keep as a state monopoly both mining and commerce (in minerals).

Thus taxes (*mukhasangraha*) on all commodities intended for sale shall be prescribed once for all.

XIII. SUPERINTENDENT OF GOLD IN THE GOLDSMITH'S OFFICE.

IN order to manufacture gold and silver jewellry, each being kept apart, the superintendent of gold shall have a goldsmiths office (*akshasála*) consisting of four rooms and one door.

In the centre of the high road a trained, skilful goldsmith of high birth and of reliable character shall be appointed to hold his shop.

Jámbúnada, that which is the product of the river, *Jambu*; *Sátakumbha*, that which is extracted from the mountain of *Satakumba*; *Hátaka*, that which is extracted from the mines known as *Hátaka*; *Vainava*, that which is the product of the mountain, *Vénu*; and *Sringasúktija*, that which is extracted from *sringasúkti* (?) are the varieties of gold.

(Gold may be obtained) either pure or amalgamated with mercury or silver or alloyed with other impurities as mine gold (*ákaródgata*).

That which is of the colour of the petals of a lotus, ductile, glossy, incapable of making any continuous sound (*anádi*), and glittering is the best; that which is reddish yellow (*raktapíta*) is of middle quality; and that which is red is of low quality.

Impure gold is of whitish colour. It shall be fused with lead of four times the quantity of the impurity. When gold is rendered brittle owing to its contamination with lead, it shall be heated with dry cowdung (*sushkapatala*). When it splits into pieces owing to hardness, it shall be drenched (after heating) into oil mixed with cowdung (*taila-gomaye*).

Mine gold which is brittle owing to its contamination with lead shall be heated wound round with cloth (*pákapatráni kritvá*); and hammered on a wooden anvil. Or it may be drenched in the mixture made of mushroom and *vajrakhanda*(*Antiquorum*).

Tutthodgata, what which is extracted from the mountain, *Tuttha*; *gaudika*, that which is the product of the country known as *Gauda*; *kámbuka*, that which is extracted from the mountain, *Kambu*; and *chákraválika*, that which is extracted from the mountain *Chakravála* are the varieties of silver.

Silver which is white, glossy, and ductile is the best; and that which is of the reverse quality is bad.

Impure silver shall be heated with lead of one-fourth the quantity of the impurity.

That which becomes full of globules, white, glowing, and of the colour of curd is pure.

When the streak of pure gold (made on touch-stone) is of the colour of turmeric, it is termed suvarna. When from one to sixteen *kákanis* of gold in a *suvarna* (of sixteen *máshakas*) are replaced by from one to sixteen *kákanis* of copper, so that the copper is inseparably alloyed with the whole mass of the remaining quantity of the gold, the sixteen varieties (carats) of the standard of the purity of gold (*shodasavarnakáh*) will be obtained.

Having first made a streak with suvarna on a touchstone, then (by the side of the streak) a streak with a piece of the gold (to be compared with it) shall be made.

Whenever a uniform streak made on the even surface of a touch-stone can be wiped off or swept away or when the streak is due to the sprinkling of any glittering powder (*gairika*) by the nail on touch-stone, then an attempt for deception can be inferred.

If, with the edge of the palm dipped in a solution, of vermilion (*játihinguláka*) or of sulphate of iron (*pushpakásísa*) in cow's urine, gold (suvarna) is touched, it becomes white.

A touch-stone with soft and shining splendour is the best. The touch-stone of the Kálinga country with the colour of green beans is also the best. A touch-stone of even or uniform colour is good in sale or purchase (of gold). That which possesses the colour of an elephant, tinged with green colour and capable of reflecting light (*pratirági*) is good in selling gold. That which is hard, durable, and of uneven colour and not reflecting light, is good for purchasers (*krayahitah*). That which is grey, greasy, of uniform colour, soft, and glossy is the best.

That (gold) which, when heated, keeps the same colour (*tápo bahirantascha samah*), is as glittering as tender sprouts, or of the colour of the flower of *kárandaka* (?) is the best.

That which is black or blue (in gold) is the impurity (*apráptaka*).

We shall deal with the balance and weights under the "Superintendent of Weights and Measures" (Chap. XIX, Book II). In accordance with the instructions given thereunder silver and gold (*rúpyasuvarnam*) may be given in exchange.

No person who is not an employee shall enter the gold-smiths' office. Any person who so enters shall be beheaded (*uchchhedyah*).

Any workman who enters the office with gold or silver shall have to forfeit the same.

Goldsmiths who are engaged to prepare various kinds of ornaments such as *kánchana* (pure gold), *prishita* (hollow ornaments), *tvashtri* (setting gems in gold) and *tapaníya*; as well as blowers and sweepers shall enter into or exit from the office after their person and dress are thoroughly examined. All of their instruments together with their unfinished work shall be left where they have been at work. That amount of gold which they have received and the ornamental work which they were doing shall be put in the centre of the office. (Finished articles) shall be examined both morning and evening and be locked up with the seal of both the manufacturer and the superintendent (*kárayatri*, the owner getting the articles prepared).

Kshepana, *guna*, and *kshudra* ate three kinds of ornamental work.

Setting jewels (*kácha*, glass bead) in gold is termed *kshepana*.

Thread-making or string making is called *guna*.

Solid work (*ghana*), hollow work (*sushira*), and the manufacture of globules furnished with a rounded orifice is what is termed *kshudra*, low or ordinary work.

For setting jewels in gold, five parts of *káñchana* (pure gold) and ten parts of gold alloyed with four parts of copper or silver shall be the required quantity (*mána*). Here the pure gold shall be preserved from the impure gold.

For setting jewels in hollow ornaments (*prishitakácha karmanah*), three parts of gold to hold the jewel and four parts for the bottom (shall be the required quantity).

For the work of *tvashtri*, copper and gold shall be mixed in equal quantities.

For silver article either solid or hollow, silver may be mixed with half of the amount of gold; or by making use of the powder or solution of vermilion, gold equal to one-fourth the amount of silver of the ornament may be painted (*vásayet*) on it.

Pure and glittering gold is *tapaníya*. This combined with an equal quantity of lead and heated with rock-salt (*saindhav'ika*) to melting point under dry cowdung becomes the basis of gold alloys of blue, red, white, yellow (*harita*), parrot and pidgeon colours.

The colouring ingredient of gold is one *kákaní* of *tíkshna* which is of the colour of the neck of a peacock, tinged with white, and which is dazzling and full of copper (*pitapúrnitam*).

Pure or impure silver (*tára*) may be heated four times with *asthituttha* (copper sulphate mixed with powdered bone), again four times with an equal quantity of lead, again four times with dry copper sulphate (*sushkatuttha*) again three times in skull (*kapála*), and lastly twice in cowdung. Thus the silver acted upon seventeen times by *tuttha* (*shodasatutthátikrántam*) and lastly heated to white light with rock salt may be made to alloy with *suvarna* to the extent of from one *kákani* to two *Máshas*. Then the *suvarna* attains white colour and is called *sveta-tára*.

When three parts of *tapaníya* (pure gold) are melted with thirty-two parts of *sveta-tára*, the compound becomes reddish white (*svetalohitakam*). When three parts of *tapaníya* are combined with thirty-two parts of copper, the compound becomes yellow (*píta*, red!). Also when three parts of the colouring ingredient (*rágatribhága*, *i.e.*, *tíkshna* referred to above) are heated with *tapaníya*, the compound becomes yellowish red (*píta*). When two parts of *sveta-tár*a and one part of*tapaníya* are heated, the whole mass becomes as green as *mudga* (*Phraseolus Mungo*). When *tapaníya* is drenched in a solution of half the quantity of black iron (*káláyasa*), it becomes black.

When *tapaníya* is twice drenched in (the above) solution mixed with mercury (*rasa*), it acquires the colour of the feathers of a parrot.

Before these varieties of gold are put to use, their test streak shall be taken on touch-stone. The process of assaying *tíkshna* and copper shall be well understood. Hence the various counterweights (*avaneyimána*) used in weighing diamonds, rubies, pearls, corals, and coins, (*rúpa*), as well as the proportional amount of gold and silver necessary for various kinds of ornaments can be well understood.

Uniform in colour, equal in the colour of test streak to the standard gold, devoid of hollow bulbs, ductile (*sthira*), very smooth, free from alloys, pleasing when worn as an ornament, not dazzling though glittering, sweet in its uniformity of mass, and pleasing the mind and eyes,---these are the qualities of *tapaníya*, pure gold.

XIV. THE DUTIES OF THE STATE GOLDSMITH IN THE HIGH ROAD.

THE State Goldsmith shall employ artisans to manufacture gold and silver coins (*rúpyasuvarna*) from the bullion of citizens and country people.

The artisans employed in the office shall do their work as ordered and in time. When under the excuse that time and nature of the work has not been prescribed, they spoil the work, they shall not only forfeit their wages, but also pay a fine of twice the amount of their wages. When they postpone work, they shall forfeit one-fourth the amount of their wages and pay a fine of twice the amount of the forfeited wages.

(The goldsmith of the mint) shall return (to the owners coins or ornaments) of the same weight, and of the same quality (*varna*) as that of the bullion (*nikshepa*) which they received (at the mint). With the exception of those (coins) which have been worn out or which have undergone diminution (*kshínaparisírna*), they shall receive the same coins (back into the mint) even after the lapse of a number of years.

The state goldsmith shall gather from the artisans employed in the mint information concerning pure gold, metallic mass (*pudgala*), coins (*lakshana*), and rate of exchange (*prayóga*).

In getting a *suvarna* coin (of 16 *máshas*) manufactured from gold or from silver, one *kákani* (one-fourth *másha*) weight of the metal more shall be given to the mint towards the loss in manufacture.

The colouring ingredient (*rágaprakshépa*) shall be two *kákanis* of *tíkshna* (copper sulphate ?) one-sixth of which will be lost during the manufacture.

When the quality (*varna*) of a coin less than the standard of a *másha* is lowered, the artisans (concerned) shall be punished with the first amercement. When its weight is less than the standard weight, they shall be punished with the middlemost amercement. Deception in balance or weights shall be punished with the highest amercement. Deception in the exchange of manufactured coins (*kritabhándopadhau*) shall also be punished with the highest amercement.

Whoever causes (gold or silver articles) to be manufactured in any place other than the mint or without being noticed by the state goldsmith shall be fined 12 *panás*, while the artisan who does that work shall, if found out, be punished with twice the above fine. If he is not found out, measures such as are described in Book IV shall be taken to detect him. When thus detected, he shall be fined 200 *panás* or shall have his fingers cut off.

Weighing balance and counterweights shall be purchased from the superintendent in charge of them. Otherwise a fine of 12 *panás* shall be imposed.

Compact work (*ghana*), compact and hollow work (*ghanasushira*), soldering (*samyúhya*), amalgamation (*avalepya*), enclosing (*samghátya*), and gilding (*vásitakam*) are the various kinds of artisan work (*kárukasma*).

False balances (*tulávishama*), removal (*apasárana*), dropping (*visrávana*), folding (*petaka*), and confounding (*pinka*) are the several means employed by goldsmiths to deceive the public.

False balance are—that of bending arms (*sannámini*); that of high helm or pivot (*utkarnika*); that of broken head (*bhinnamastaka*); that of hollow neck (*upakanthi*); that of bad strings (*kusikya*); that of bad cups or pans (*sakatukakshya*); that which is crooked or shaking (*párivellya*); and that which is combined with a magnet (*ayaskánta*).

When, by what is called *Triputaka* which consists of two parts of silver and one part of copper, an equal portion of pure alluvial gold is replaced, that deceitful act is termed copper-removal (*triputaká-*

vasáritam); when, by copper, an equal portion of gold is replaced, that act is termed copper-removal (*sulbávasáritam*); when by *vellakaan* equal portion of gold is replaced, it is termed *vellaka*-removal; and when pure alluvial gold is replaced by that gold half of which is mixed with copper, it is termed gold removal (*hemávasáritam*).

A crucible with a base metallic piece hidden in it; metallic excrement; pincers; a pair of tongs; metallic pieces (*jongani*); and borax (*sauvarchikálavanam*),—these are the several things which are made use of by goldsmiths in stealing gold.

When, intentionally causing the crucible (containing the bullion) to burst, a few sandlike particles of the metal are picked up along with other particles of a base metal previously put therein, and the whole is wrought into a mass for the intended coin or ornament), this act is termed dropping (*visravana*); or when examining the folded or inlaid leaves of an ornament (*áchitakapatrapariksháyám*) deception is perpetrated by substituting silver for gold, or when particles of a base metal are substituted for those of gold, it is termed dropping (*visrávana*) likewise.

Folding (*petaka*) either firm (*gádha*) or loose (*abhyuddhárya*) is practiced in soldering, in preparing amalgams, and in enclosing (a piece of base metal with two pieces of a superior metal).

When a lead piece (*sísarúpa*--lead coin) is firmly covered over with gold leaf by means of wax (*ashtaka*), that act is termed *gádhapetaka*, firm folding; and when the same is loosely folded, it is termed loose folding.

In amalgams, a single or double layer (of a superior metal) is made to cover a piece (of base metal). Copper or silver may also be placed between two leaves (of a superior metal). A copper piece (*sulbarúpya*) may be covered over with gold leaf, the surface and the edges being smoothened; similarly a piece of any base metal may be covered over with double leaf of copper or silver, the surface and the edges being smoothened.

The two forms of folding may be detected by heating, by testing on touch-stone (*nikasha*) or by observing absence of sound when it is rubbed (*nissabdollekhana*).

(They) find out loose folding in the acid juice of *badarámla* (*Flacourtia Cataphracta* or jujube fruit) or in salt water;—so much for folding (*petaka*).

In a compact and hollow piece (*ghana-sushire rúpe*), small particles of gold-like mud (*suvarnamrinválukáh*) or bit of vermilion (*hingulakalkah*) are so heated as to make them firmly adhere to the piece inside. Even in a compact piece (*dridhavástuke rúpe*), the waxlike mud of *Gándhára* mixed with the particles of goldlike sand is so heated as to adhere to the piece. These two kinds of impurities are got rid of by hammering the pieces when red hot.

In an ornament or a coin (*sapari-bhánde vá rúpe*) salt mixed with hard sand (*katusarkará*) is so heated in flame as to make it firmly adhere to (the ornament or coin). This (salt and sand) can be got rid of by boiling (*kváthana*).

In some pieces, mica may be firmly fixed inside by wax and covered over with a double leaf (of gold or silver). When such a piece with mica or glass inside is suspended in water (*udake*) one of its sides dips more than the other; or when pierced by a pin, the pin goes very easily in the layers of mica in the interior (*pataláantareshu*).

Spurious stones and counterfeit gold and silver may be substituted for real ones in compact and hollow pieces (*ghanasushira*). They are detected by hammering the pieces when red hot---so much for confounding (*pinka*).

Hence (the state goldsmith) shall have a thorough knowledge of the species, characteristics, colour, weight, and formation (*pudgala-lakshana*) of diamonds, precious stones (*mani*), pearls, corals and coins (*rúpa*).

There are four ways of deception perpetrated when examining new pieces or repairing old ones: they are hammering, cutting, scratching and rubbing.

When, under the excuse of detecting the deception known as folding (*petaka*) in hollow pieces or in threads or in cups (made of gold or silver), the articles in question are hammered, that act is termed hammering.

When a lead piece (covered over with gold or silver leaf) is substituted for a real one and its interior is cut off, it is termed cutting (avachchhedanam).

When compact pieces are scratched by *tíkshna* (copper sulphate ?), that act is termed scratching (*ullekhana*).

When, by a piece of cloth painted with the powder of sulphuret of arsenic (*haritála*), red arsenic (*manassila*), or vermilion or with the powder of *kuruvinda* (black salt ?), gold or silver articles are rubbed, that act is termed rubbing.

By these acts, gold and silver articles (*bhándáni*) undergo diminution; but no other kind of injury is done to them.

In all those pieces which are hammered, cut, scratched, or rubbed the loss can be inferred by comparing them with intact pieces of similar description. In amalgamated pieces (*avalepya*) which are cut off, the loss can be ascertained by cutting off an equal portion of a similar piece. Those pieces the appearance of which has changed shall be often heated and drenched in water.

(The state goldsmith) shall infer deception (*kácham vidyát*) when [the artisan preparing articles pays undue attention to] throwing away, counter-weight, fire, anvil (*gandika*), working instruments (*bhandika*), the seat (*adhikarani*), the assaying balance, folds of dress (*chellachollakam*), his head, his thigh, flies, eagerness to look at his own body, the water-pot, and the firepot.

Regarding silver, bad smell like that of rotten meat, hardness due to any alloy (*mala*), projection (*prastína*), and bad colour may be considered as indicating adulteration.

Thus articles (of gold and silver) new or old, or of bad or unusual colour are to be examined and adequate fines as described above shall be imposed.

XV. THE SUPERINTENDENT OF STOREHOUSE.

THE superintendent of storehouse (*Koshthágára*) shall supervise the accounts of agricultural produce (*síta*); taxes coming under *Ráshtra*, country-parts; commerce (*krayima*); barter (*parivartna*); begging for grains (*prámityaka*); grains borrowed with promise to repay (*ápamityaka*); manufacture of rice, oils, etc. (*simhanika*); accidental revenue (*anyajáta*); statements to check expenditure (*vyayapratyaya*); and recovery of past arrears (*upasthánam*).

Whatever in the shape of agricultural produce is brought in by the superintendent of agriculture, (of crown-lands) is termed *sítá*.

The taxes that are fixed (*pindakara*), taxes that are paid in the form of one-sixth of produce (*shadbhága*), provision paid (by the people) for the army (*senábhakta*), taxes that are levied for religious purposes (*bali*), taxes or subsidies that are paid by vassal kings and others (*kara*), taxes that are specially collected on the occasion of the birth of a prince (*utsanga*), taxes that are collected when there is some margin left for such collection (*pársva*), compensation levied in the shape of grains for any damage done by cattle to crops (*párihínaka*), presentation made to the king, (*aupáyanika*), and taxes that are levied on lands below tanks, lakes, etc., built by the king (*Kaushtheyaka*),--all these come under the head '*Ráshtra*.'

Sale proceeds of grains, grains purchased and the collection of interest in kind or grain debts (*prayogapratyádána*) are termed commerce.

Profitable exchange of grains for grains is termed barter (*parivarthana*).

Grains collected by begging is termed *prámityaka*.

Grains borrowed with promise to repay the same is termed *ápamityaka*.

Pounding (rice, etc.), dividing (pulses, etc.), frying (corns and beans), manufacture of beverages (*suktakarma*), manufacture of flour by employing those persons who live upon such works, extracting oil by employing shepherds and oil-makers, and manufacture of sugar from the juice of sugar-cane are termed *simhanika*.

Whatever is lost and forgotten (by others) and the like form accidental revenue (*anyajáta*).

Investment, the relic of a wrecked undertaking, and savings from an estimated outlay are the means to check expenditure (*vyayapratyaya*).

That amount or quantity of compensation which is claimed for making use of a different balance or for any error in taking a handful is termed *vyáji*.

Collection of arrears is termed '*upastháno*,' 'recovery of past arrears.'

Of grains, oils, sugar, and salt, all that concerns grains will be treated of in connection with the duties of the 'Superintendent of Agriculture.'

Clarified butter, oil, serum of flesh, and pith or sap (of plants, etc.)., are termed oils (*sneha*).

Decoction (*phánita*), jaggory, granulated sugar, and sugar-candy are termed *kshára*.

Saindhava, that which is the product of the country of *Sindhu*; *Sámudra*, that which is produced from seawater; *Bida*; *Yavakshara*, *nitre*, *Sauvarchala*, that which is the product of the country of *suvarchala*; and *udbhedaja*, that which is extracted from saline soil are termed *lavana*, salt.

The honey of the bee as well as the juice extracted from grapes is called *madhu*.

Mixture made by combining any one of the substances, such as the juice of sugar-cane, jaggory, honey,. the, juice of grapes, the essence of the fruits of *jambu* (*Euginia Jambolana*) and of *jaka* tree—with the essence of *meshasringa* (a kind of plant) and long pepper, with or without the addition of the essence of *chirbhita* (a kind of gourd), cucumber, sugar-cane, mango-fruit and the fruit of *myrobalam*, the mixture being prepared so as to last for a month, or six months, or a year, constitute the group of astringents (*sukta-varga*).

The fruits of those trees which bear acid fruits, those of *karamarda* (*Carissa Carandas*),those of *vidalámalka* (*myrobalam*), those of *matulanga* (citron tree), those of kola (small jujuba), those of *badara* (*Flacourtia Cataphracta*), those of*sauvíra* (big jujuba), and those of *parushaka* (*Grewia Asiatica*) and the like come under the group of acid fruits.

Curds, acid prepared from grains and the like are acids in liquid form.

Long pepper, black pepper, ginger, cumin seed, *kiratatikta* (*Agathotes Chirayta*), white mustard, coriander, *choraka* (a plant), *damanaka* (*Artemisia Indica*), *maruvaka* (*Vangueria Spinosa*), *sigru* (*Hyperanthera Moringa*), and the like together with their roots (*kánda*) come under the group of pungent substances (*tiktavarga*).

Dried fish, bulbous roots (*kándamúla*), fruits and vegetables form the group of edibles (*sakavarga*).

Of the store, thus, collected, half shall be kept in reserve to ward off the calamities of the people and only the other half shall be used. Old collection shall be replaced by new supply.

The superintendent shall also personally supervise the increase or diminution sustained in grains when they are pounded (*kshunna*), or frayed (*ghrishta*), or reduced to flour (*pishta*), or fried (*bhrashta*), or dried after soaking in water.

The essential part (*sára, i.e.*, that which is fit for food) of *kodrava* (*Paspalam Scrobiculatum*) and of *vrihi* (rice) is one-half; that of *sáli* (a kind of rice) is (half) less by one-eighth part; that of *varaka* (*Phraseolus Trilobus*) is (half) less by one-third part; that of *priyangu* (panic seed or millet) is one-half ; that of *chamasi* (barley), of *mudga* (*Phraseolus Mungo*) and of *masha* (*Phraseolus Radiatus*) is (half) less by one-eighth part; that of *saibya* (*simbi*) is one-half; that of *masúra*(*Ervum Hirsutum*) is (half) less by one-third part (than the raw material or grains from which it is prepared).

Raw flour and *kulmasha* (boiled and forced rice) will be as much as one and a half of the original quantity of the grains.

Barley gruel as well as its flour baked will be twice the original quantity.

Kodrava (*Paspalam Scrobiculatum*), *varaka* (*Phraseolus Trilobus*), *udáraka* (*Panicum*), and *priyangu* (millet) will increase three times the original quantity when cooked. *Vríhi* (rice) will increase four times when cooked. *Sáli* (a kind of rice) will increase five times when cooked.

Grains will increase twice the original quantity when moistened; and two and a half times when soaked to sprouting condition.

Grains fried will increase by one-fifth the original quantity; leguminous seeds (*kaláya*), when fried, will increase twice the original; likewise rice when fried.

Oil extracted from *atasi* (linseed) will be one-sixth (of the quantity of the seed); that extracted from the seeds, *nimba* (*Azadirachta Indica*), *kusámra* (?), and *Kapittha* (*Feronia Elephantum*) will be one-fifth; and that extracted from *tila*(seasumum), *kusumba* (a sort of kidney bean), *madhúka* (*Bassia Latifolia*), and *ingudi* (*Terminalia Catappa*) will be one-fourth.

Five *palas* of *kárpása* (cotton) and of *kshauma* (flax) will yield one *pala* of threads.

Rice prepared in such a way that five *dróna* of *sáli* yield ten *ádhakas* of rice will be fit to be the food of young elephants; eleven *ádhakas* from five *drónas* for elephants of bad temper (*vyála*); ten *ádhakas* from the same quantity for elephants trained for riding; nine *ádhakas* from the same quantity for elephants used in war; eight *ádhakas* from the same for infantry; eleven *ádhakas* from the same for chiefs of the army; six *ádhakas* from the same for queens and princes and five *ádhakas* from the same quantity for kings.

One *prastha* of rice, pure and unsplit, one-fourth *prastha* of *súpa*, and clarified butter or oil equal to one-fourth part of (*súpa*) will suffice to form one meal of an Arya.

One-sixth *prastha* of *súpa* for a man; and half the above quantity of oil will form one meal for low castes (*avara*).

The same rations less by one-fourth the above quantities will form one meal for a woman; and half the above rations for children.

For dressing twenty *palas* of flesh, half a *kutumba* of oil, one *pala* of salt, one *pala* of sugar (*kshára*), two *dharanas* of pungent substances (*katuka*, spices), and half a *prastha* of curd (will be necessary).

For dressing greater quantities of flesh, the same ingredients can be proportionally increased.

For cooking *sákas* (dried fish and vegetables), the above substances are to be added one and a half times as much.

For dressing dried fish, the above ingredients are to be added twice as much.

Measures of rations for elephants and horses will be described in connection with the "Duties of Their Respective Superintendents."

For bullocks, one *drona* of *masha* (*Phraseolus Radiatus*) or one *drona* of barley cooked with other things, as prescribed for horses, is the requisite quantity of food, besides the special and additional provision of one *tula* of oilcakes (*ghánapinyaka*) or ten *ádhakas* of bran (*kanakuttana-kundaka*).

Twice the above quantity for buffaloes and camels.

Half a *drona* for asses, red spotted deer and deer with white stripes.

One *ádhaka* for an antelope and big red deer.

Half an *ádhaka* or one *ádhaka* of grain together with bran for a goat, a ram and a boar.

One *prastha* of cooked rice for dogs.

Half a *prastha* for a *hamsa* (goose), a *krauncha* (heron) and a peacock.

From the above, the quantity of rations enough for one meal for other beasts, cattle, birds, and rogue elephants (*vyála*) may be inferred.

Charcoal and chaff may be given over for iron smelting and lime-kiln (*bhittilepya*).

Bran and flour (*kánika*) may be given to slaves, labourers, and cooks. The surplus of the above may be given to those who prepare cooked rice, and rice-cakes.

The weighing balance, weights, measures, mill-stone (*rochani*), pestle, mortar, wooden contrivances for pounding rice, etc., (*kuttakayantra*), contrivances for splitting seeds into pieces (*rochakayantra*), winnowing fans, sieves (*chálani*) grain-baskets (*kandoli*), boxes, and brooms are the necessary instruments.

Sweepers; preservers; those who weigh things (*dharaka*); those who measure grains, etc.; those who supervise the work of measuring grains (*mápaka*); those who supervise the supply of commodities to the store-house (*dápaka*); those who supply commodities (*dáyaka*); those who are employed to receive compensation for any real or supposed error in measuring grains, etc. (*sálákáipratigráhaka*); slaves; and labourers;—all these are called *vishti*.

Grains are heaped up on the floor; jaggory (*kshára*) is bound round in grass-rope (*múta*); oils are kept in earthenware or wooden vessels; and salt is heaped up on the surface of the ground.

XVI. THE SUPERINTENDENT OF COMMERCE.

THE Superintendent of Commerce shall ascertain demand or absence of demand for, and rise or fall in the price of, various kinds of merchandise which may be the products either of land or of water and which may have been brought in either by land or by water path. He shall also ascertain the time suitable for their distribution, centralisation, purchase, and sale.

That merchandise which is widely distributed shall be centralised and its price enhanced. When the enhanced rate becomes popular, another rate shall be declared.

That merchandise of the king which is of local manufacture shall be centralised; imported merchandise shall be distributed in several markets for sale. Both kinds of merchandise shall be favourably sold to the people.

He shall avoid such large profits as will harm the people.

There shall be no restriction to the time of sale of those commodities for which there is frequent demand; nor shall they be subject to the evils of centralisation (*sankuladosha*).

Or pedlars may sell the merchandise of the king at a fixed price in many markets and pay necessary compensation (*vaidharana*) proportional to the loss entailed upon it (*chhedánurúpam*).

The amount of *vyáji* due on commodities sold by cubical measure is one-sixteenth of the quantity (*shodasabhágo mánavyáji*); that on commodities sold by weighing balance is one-twentieth of the quantity; and that on commodities sold in numbers is one-eleventh of the whole.

The superintendent shall show favour to those who import foreign merchandise: mariners (*návika*) and merchants who import foreign merchandise shall be favoured with remission of the trade-taxes, so that they may derive some profit (*áyatikshamam parihάram dadyát*).

Foreigners importing merchandise shall be exempted from being sued for debts unless they are (local) associations and partners.

Those who sell the merchandise of the king shall invariably put their sale proceeds in a wooden box kept in a fixed place and provided with a single aperture on the top.

During the eighth part of the day, they shall submit to the superintendent the sale report, saying "this much has been sold and this much remains;" they shall also hand over the weights and measures. Such are the rules applicable to local traffic.

As regards the sale of the king's merchandise in foreign countries:---

Having ascertained the value of local produce as compared with that of foreign produce that can be obtained in barter, the superintendent will find out (by calculation) whether there is any margin left for profit after meeting the payments (to the foreign king) such as the toll (*sulka*), road-cess (*vartaní*), conveyance-cess (*átiváhika*), tax payable at military stations (*gulmadeya*), ferry-charges (*taradeya*), subsistence to the merchant and his followers (*bhakta*), and the portion of merchandise payable to the foreign king (*bhága*).

If no profit can be realised by selling the local produce in foreign countries, he has to consider whether any local produce can be profitably bartered for any foreign produce. Then he may send one quarter of his valuable merchandise through safe roads to different markets on land. In view of large profits, he (the deputed merchant) may make friendship with the forest-guards, boundary-guards, and officers in charge of cities and of country-parts (of the foreign king). He shall take care to secure his treasure (*sára*) and life from danger. If he cannot reach the intended market, he may sell the merchandise (at any market) free from all dues (*sarvadeyavisuddham*).

Or he may take his merchandise to other countries through rivers (*nadípatha*).

He shall also gather information as to conveyance-charges (*yánabhágaka*), subsistence on the way (*pathyadana*), value of foreign merchandise that can be obtained in barter for local merchandise, occasions of pilgrimages (*yátrakála*), means that can be employed to ward off dangers (of the journey), and the history of commercial towns (*panyapattanachháritra*).

Having gathered information as to the transaction in commercial towns along the banks of rivers, he shall transport his merchandise to profitable markets and avoid unprofitable ones.

XVII. THE SUPERINTENDENT OF FOREST PRODUCE.

THE Superintendent of Forest Produce shall collect timber and other products of forests by employing those who guard productive forests. He shall not only start productive works in forests, but also fix adequate fines and compensations to be levied from those who cause any damage to productive forests except in calamities.

The following are forest products.

Sáka (teak), *tinisa* (Dalbergia Ougeinensis), *dhanvana* (?), *arjuna* (Terminalia Arjuna), *madhúka* (Bassia Latifolia), *tilaka* (Barleria Cristata), *tála* (palmyra), *simsúpa* (Dalbergia Sissu), *arimeda* (Fetid Mimosa), *rájádana* (Mimosops Kauki), *sirisha* (Mimosa Sirísha), *khad ira* (Mimosa Catechu), *sarala* (Pinus Longifolia), *tálasarja* (*sal* tree or Shorea Robesta), *asvakarna* (Vatica Robesta), *somavalka* (a kind of white *khadíra*), *kasámra* (?), *priyaka* (yellow *sal* tree), *dhava*(Mimos a Hexandra), etc., are the trees of strong timber (*sáradáruvarga*).

Utaja, *Chimiya*, *Chava*, *Vénu*, *Vamsa*, *Sátina*, *Kantaka*, and *Bháll úka*, etc., form the group of bamboo.

Vetra (cane), sokavalli, vási (Justicia Ganderussa?), syámalatá (Ic hnocarpus), nágalata (betel), etc., form the group of creepers.

Málati (Jasminum Grandiflorum), *dúrvá* (panic grass), *arka* (Calo tropis Gigantea), *sana* (hemp), *gavedhuka* (Coix Barbata), *atasí* (Linu m Usitatis simum), etc., form the group of fibrous plants (*valkavarga*).

Munja (Saccharum Munja), *balbaja* (Eleusine Indica), etc., are plants which yield rope-making material (*rajjubhánda*).

Táli (Corypha Taliera), *tála* (palmyra or Borassus Flabelliformis), and *bhúrja* (birch) yield leaves (*patram*).

Kimsuka (Butea Frondosa), *kusumbha* (Carthamus Tinctorius), and *kumkuma* (Crocus Sativus) yield flowers.

Bulbous roots and fruits are the group of medicines.

Kálakúta, *Vatsanábha*, *Háláhala*, *Meshasringa*, *Mustá*, (Cypers Rotundus), *kushtha*, *mahávisha*, *vellitaka*, *gaurárdra*, *bálaka*, *márka ta, haimavata, kálingaka, daradaka, kolasáraka, ushtraka,* etc., are poisons.

Likewise snakes and worms kept in pots are the group of poisons.Skins are those of *godha* (alligator), *seraka* (?), *dvípi* (leopar d), *simsumára* (porpoise), *simha* (lion), *vyághra* (tiger), *hasti*, (elepha nt.), *mahisha* (buffalo), *chamara* (bos grunniens), *gomriga* (bos gavaeus), and *gavaya* (the *gayal*).

Bones, bile (*pittha*), *snáyu* (?), teeth, horn, hoofs, and tails of the above animals as well as of other beasts, cattle, birds and snakes (*vyála*).

Káláyasa (iron), *támra* (copper), *vritta* (?), *kámsya* (bronze), *sísa* (lead), *trapu* (tin), *vaikrintaka* (mercury ?), and *árakuata* (brass), are metals.Utensils (*bhanda*), are those made of cane, bark (*vidala*), and clay (*mrittiká*).

Charcoal, bran, and ashes are other things. Menageries of beasts, cattle, and birds.Collection of firewood and fodder.

The superintendent of forest produce shall carry on either inside or outside (the capital city) the manufacture of all kinds of articles which are necessary for life or for the defence of forts.

XVIII. THE SUPERINTENDENT OF THE ARMOURY.

THE Superintendent of the Armoury shall employ experienced workmen of tried ability to manufacture in a given time and for fixed wages wheels, weapons, mail armour, and other accessory instruments for use in battles, in the construction or defence of forts, or in destroying the cities or strongholds of enemies.

All these weapons and instruments shall be kept in places suitably prepared for them. They shall not only be frequently dusted and transferred from one place to another, but also be exposed to the sun. Such weapons as are likely to be affected by heat and vapour (*úshmopasneha*) and to be eaten by worms shall be kept in safe localities. They shall also be examined now and then with reference to the class to which they belong, their forms, their characteristics, their size, their source, their value, and their total quantity.

Sarvatobhadra, *jamadagnya*, *bahumukha*, *visvásagháti*, *samghá ti*, *yánaka*, *parjanyaka*, *ardhabáhu*, and *úrdhvabáhu* are immoveable machines (*sthirayantrám*).

Pánchálika, *devadanda*, *súkarika*, *musala*, *yashti*, *hastiváraka*, *t álavrinta*, *mudgara*, *gada*, *spriktala*, *kuddála*, *ásphátima*, *audhgháti ma*, *sataghni*, *trisúla*, and *chakra* are moveable machines.

Sakti, *prása*, *kunta*, *hátaka*, *bhindivála*, *súla*, *tomara*, *varáhakar na*, *kanaya*, *karpana*, *trásika*, and the like are weapons with edges like a ploughshare (*halamukháni*).

Bows made of *tála* (palmyra), of *chápa* (a kind of bamboo), of *dáru* (a kind of wood), and *sringa* (bone or horn) are respectively called *kármuka*, *kodanda*, *druna*, and *dhanus*.

Bow-strings are made of *múrva* (Sansviera Roxburghiana), *arka* (Catotropis Gigantea), *sána* (hemp), *gavedhu* (Coix Barbata), *venu* (bamboo bark), and *snáyu* (sinew).

Venu, *sara*, *saláka*, *dandásana*, and *nárácha* are different kinds of arrows. The edges of arrows shall be so made of iron, bone or wood as to cut, rend or pierce.

Nistrimsa, *mandalágra*, and *asiyashti* are swords. The handles of swords are made of the horn of rhinoceros, buffalo, of the tusk of elephants, of wood, or of the root of bamboo.

Parasu, *kuthára*, *pattasa*, *khanitra*, *kuddála*, *chakra*, and *kándachchhedana* are razor-like weapons.

Yantrapáshána, *goshpanapáshána*, *mushtipáshána*, *rochaní* (mi ll-stone), and stones are other weapons (*áyudháni*).

Lohajáliká, *patta*, *kavacha*, and *sútraka* are varieties of armour made of iron or of skins with hoofs and horns of porpoise, rhinoceros, bison, elephant or cow.

Likewise *sirastrána* (cover for the head), *kanthatrána* (cover for the neck) *kúrpása* (cover for the trunk), *kanchuka* (a coat extending as far as the knee joints), *váravána* (a coat extending as far as the heels), *patta*, (a coat without cover for the arms), and *nágodariká* (gloves) are varieties of armour.

Veti, charma, hastikarna, tálamúla, dharmanika, kaváta, kitika, apratihata, and *valáhakánta* are instruments used in self-defence (*ávaranáni*).

Ornaments for elephants, chariots, and horses as well as goads and hooks to lead them in battle-fields constitute accessory things (*upakaranáni*).

(Besides the above) such other delusive and destructive contrivances (as are treated of in Book XIV) together with any other new inventions of expert workmen (shall also be kept in stock.)

The Superintendent of Armoury shall precisely ascertain the demand and supply of weapons, their application, their wear and tear, as well as their decay and loss.

XIX. THE SUPERINTENDENT OF WEIGHTS AND MEASURES.

THE Superintendent of Weights and Measures shall have the same manufactured.

10 seeds of *másha* (*Phraseolus Radiatus*) or	
5 ,, *gunja* (*Cabrus Precatorius*)	= 1 *suvarna-másha*.
16 *máshas*	= 1 *suvarna* or *karsha*.
4 *karshas*	= 1 *pala*.
88 white mustard seeds	= 1 silver-*másha*.
16 silver *mashas* or 20 *saibya* seeds	= 1 *dharana*.
20 grains of rice	= 1 *dharana* of a diamond.

Ardha-másha (half a *másha*), one *másha*, two *máshas*, four *máshas*, eight *máshas*, one *suvarna*, two *suvarnas*, four *suvarnas*, eight *suvarnas*, ten *suvarnas*, twenty *suvarnas*, thirty *suvarnas*, forty *suvarnas* and one hundred *suvarnas* are different units of weights.

Similar series of weights shall also be made in *dharanas*.

Weights (*pratimánáni*) shall be made of iron or of stones available in the countries of Magadha and Mekala; or of such things as will neither contract when wetted, nor expand under the influence of heat.

Beginning with a lever of six *angulas* in length and of one *pala* in the weight of its metallic mass, there shall be made ten (different) balances with levers successively increasing by one *pala* in the weight of their metallic masses, and by eight *angulas* in their length. A scale-pan shall be attached to each of them on one or both sides.

A balance called *samavrittá*, with its lever 72-angulas long and weighing 53 *palas* in its metallic mass shall also be made. A scalepan of 5 *palas* in the weight of its metallic mass being attached to its edge, the horizontal position of the lever (*samakarana*) when weighing a *karsha* shall be marked (on that part of the lever where, held by a thread, it stands horizontal). To the left of that mark, symbols such as 1 *pala*, 12, 15 and 20 *palas* shall be marked. After that, each place of tens up to 100 shall be marked. In the place of *Akshas*, the sign of *Nándi* shall be marked.

Likewise a balance called *parimání* of twice as much metallic mass as that of *samavrittá* and of 96 *angulas* in length shall be made. On its lever, marks such as 20, 50 and 100 above its initial weight of 100 shall be carved.

20 *tulas*	== 1 *bhára*.
10 *dharanas*	== 1 *pala*.
100 such *palas*	== 1 *áyamání* (measure of royal income).

Public balance (*vyávaháriká*), servants' balance (*bhájiní*), and harem balance (*antahpurabhájiní*) successively decrease by five *palas* (compared with *áyamáni*).

A *pala* in each of the above successively falls short of the same in *áyamáni* by half a *dharana*. The metallic mass of the levers of each of the above successively decreases in weight by two ordinary *palas* and in length by six *angulas*.

Excepting flesh, metals, salt, and precious stones, an excess of five *palas* (*prayáma*) of all other commodities (shall be given to the king) when they are weighed in the two first-named balances.

A wooden balance with a lever 8 hands long, with measuring marks and counterpoise weights shall be erected on a pedestal like that of a peacock.

Twenty-five *palas* of firewood will cook one *prastha* of rice.

This is the unit (for the calculation) of any greater or less quantity (of firewood).

Thus weighing balance and weights are commented upon.

Then,

200 *palas* in the grains of *másha*	1 *drona* which is an *áyamána*, a measure of royal income.
187½ ,,	1 public *drona*.
175 ,,	1 *bhájaníya*, servants' measure
162½ ,,	1 *antahpurabhájaníya*, harem measure.

Adhaka, *prastha*, and *kudumba*, are each ¼ of the one previously mentioned.

16 *dronas*	== 1 *várí*.
20 ,,	== 1 *kumbha*.
10 *kumbhas*	== 1 *vaha*.

Cubic measures shall be so made of dry and strong wood that when filled with grains, the conically heaped-up portion of the grains standing on the mouth of the measure is equal to ¼th of the quantity of the grains (so measured); or the measures may also be so made that a quantity equal to the heaped-up portion can be contained within (the measure).

But liquids shall always be measured level to the mouth of the measure.

With regard to wine, flowers, fruits, bran, charcoal and slaked lime, twice the quantity of the heaped-up portion (*i.e.*, ¼th of the measure) shall be given in excess.

1¼ *panas*is the price of	a *drona*.
¾ *pana*	an *ádhaka*.
6 *máshas*	a *prastha*.
1 *másha*	a *kudumba*.

The price of similar liquid-measures is double the above.

20 *panas* is the price of	a set of counter-weights.
6⅔ *panas*	of a *tulá* (balance).

The Superintendent shall charge 4 *máshas* for stamping weights or measures. A fine of 27¼ *panas* shall be imposed for using unstamped weights or measures.

Traders shall every day pay one *kákaní* to the Superintendent towards the charge of stamping the weights and measures.

Those who trade in clarified butter, shall give, (to purchasers) 1/32 part more as *taptavyáji* (*i.e.*, compensation for decrease in the quantity of *ghi* owing to its liquid condition). Those who trade in oil shall give 1/64 part more as *taptavyáji*.

(While selling liquids, traders) shall give 1/50 part more as *mánasráva* (*i.e.*, compensation for diminution in the quantity owing to its overflow or adhesion to the measuring can).

Half, one-fourth, and one-eighth parts of the measure, *kumbha*, shall also be manufactured.

84 *kudumbas* of clarified butter are held to be equal to	a *wáraka* of the same;
64 *kudumbas* of clarified butter are held to be equal to	make one *wáraka* of oil (*taila*);and¼ of a *wáraka* is called *ghatika*, either of *ghi* or of

	oil.

[Thus ends Chapter XIX, "Balance, Weights and Measures" in Book II, "The Duties of Government Superintendents" of the *Arthasástra* of Kautilya. End of the fortieth chapter from the beginning.]

XX. MEASUREMENT OF SPACE AND TIME.

THE Superintendent of lineal measure shall possess the knowledge of measuring space and time.

8 atoms (*paramánavah*) are equal to	1 particle thrown off by the wheel of a chariot.
8 particles are equal to	1 *likshá*.
8 *likshás* are equal to	the middle of a *yúka* (louse) or a *yúka* of medium size.
8 *yúkas* are equal to	1 *yava* (barley) of middle size.
8 *yavas* are equal to	1 *angula* (¾ of an English inch) or the middlemost joint of the middle finger of a man of medium size may be taken to be equal to an *angula*.
4 *angulas* are equal to	1 *dhanurgraha*.
8 *angulas* are equal to	1 *dhanurmushti*.
12 *angulas* are equal to	1 *vitasti*, or 1 *chháyápaurusha*.
14 *angulas* are equal to	1 *sama*, *sala*, *pariraya*, or *pada*.
2 *vitastis* are equal to	1 *aratni* or 1 *prájápatya hasta*
2 *vitastis plus* 1 *dhanurgraha* are equal to	1 *hasta* used in measuring balances and cubic measures, and pasture lands.
2 *vitastis plus* 1 *dhanurmusti*	1 *kishku* or 1 *kamsa*.

42 *angulas* are equal to	1 *kishku* according to sawyers and blacksmiths and used in measuring the grounds for the encampment of the army, for forts and palaces.
54 *angulas* are equal to	1 *hasta* used in measuring timber forests.
84 *angulas* are equal to	1 *vyáma*, used in measuring ropes and the depth of digging, in terms of a man's height.
4 *aratnis* are equal to	1 *danda*, 1 *dhanus*, 1 *nálika* and 1 *paurusha*.
108 *angulas* are equal to	1 *garhapatya dhanus* (*i.e.*, a measure used by carpenters called *grihapati*). This measure is used in measuring roads and fort-walls.
The same (108 *angulas*) are equal to	1 *paurusha*, a measure used in building sacrificial altars.
6 *kamsas* or 192 *angulas* are equal to	1 *danda*, used in measuring such lands as are gifted to *Bráhmans*.
10 *dandas* are equal to	1 *rajju*.
2 *rajjus* are equal to	1 *paridesa* (square measure).
3 *rajjus* are equal to	1 *nivartana* (square measure).
The same (3 *rajjus*) *plus* 2 *dandas* on one side only are equal to	1 *báhu* (arm).
1000 *dhanus* are equal to	1 *goruta* (sound of a cow).
4 *gorutas* are equal to	1 *yojana*.

Thus are the lineal and square measures dealt with.

Then with regard to the measures of time: (The divisions of time are) a *truti*, *lava*, *nimesha*, *káshthá*, *kalá*, *náliká*, *muhúrta*, forenoon, afternoon, day, night, *paksha*, month, *ritu* (season), *ayana* (solstice); *samvatsara* (year), and *yuga*.

2 *trutis* are equal to	1 *lava*.
2 *lavas* are equal to	1 *nimesha*.
5 *nimeshas* are equal to	1 *káshthá*.
30 *káshthás* are equal to	1 *kalá*.
40 *kalás* are equal to	1 *náliká*, or the time during which one *ádhaka* of water passes out of a pot through an aperture of the same diameter as that of a wire of 4 *angulas* in length and made of 4*máshas* of gold.
2 *nálikas* are equal to	1 *muhúrta*.
15 *muhúrtas* are equal to	1 day or 1 night.

Such a day and night happen in the months of *Chaitra* and *Asvayuja*. Then after the period of six months it increases or diminishes by three *muhúrtas*.

When the length of shadow is eight *paurushas* (96 *angulas*), it is 1/18th part of the day.

When it is 6 *paurushas* (72 *angulas*), it is 1/14th part of the day; when 4 *paurushas*, 1/8th part; when 2 *paurushas*, 1/6th part; when 1 *paurusha*, ¼th part; when it is 8 *angulas*, 3/10th part (*trayodasabhágah*); when 4 *angulas*, 3/8th part; and when no shadow is cast, it is to be considered midday.

Likewise when the day declines, the same process in reverse order shall be observed.

It is in the month of *Ashádha* that no shadow is cast in midday. After *Ashádha*, during the six months from *Srávana* upwards, the length of shadow successively increases by two *angulas* and during the next six months from *Mágha*upwards, it successively decreases by two *angulas*.

Fifteen days and nights together make up one *paksha*. That *paksha* during which the moon waxes is white (*sukla*) and that *paksha* during which the moon wanes is *bahula*.

Two *pakshas* make one month (*mása*). Thirty days and nights together make one work-a-month (*prakarmamásah*). The same (30 days and nights) with an additional half a day makes one solar month (*saura*).

The same (30) less by half a day makes one lunar month (*chandramása*).

Twenty-seven (days and nights) make a sidereal month (*nakshatramása*).

Once in thirty-two months there comes one *malamása* profane month, *i.e.*, an extra month added to lunar year to harmonise it with the solar.

Once in thirty-five months there comes a *malamása* for *Asvaváhas*.

Once in forty months there comes a *malamása* for *hastiváhas*.

Two months make one *ritu* (season).

Srávana and *proshthapada* make the rainy season (*varshá*).

Asvayuja and *Kárthíka* make the autumn (*sarad*).

Márgasírsha and *Phausha* make the winter (*hemanta*).

Mágha and *Phalguna* make the dewy season (*sisira*).

Chaitra and *Vaisákha* make the spring (*vasanta*).

Jyeshthámúlíya and *Ashádha* make the summer (*grishma*).

Seasons from *sisira* and upwards are the summer-solstice (*uttaráyana*), and (those) from *varshá* and upwards are the winter solstice (*dakshináyana*). Two solstices (*ayanas*) make one year (*samvatsara*). Five years make one *yuga*.

The sun carries off (*harati*) 1/60th of a whole day every day and thus makes one complete day in every two months (*ritau*). Likewise the moon (falls behind by 1/60th of a whole day every day and falls behind one day in every two months). Thus in the middle of every third year, they (the sun and the moon) make one *adhimása*, additional month, first in the summer season and second at the end of five years.

XXI. THE SUPERINTENDENT OF TOLLS.

THE Superintendent of Tolls shall erect near the large gate of the city both the toll-house and its flag facing either the north or the south. When merchants with their merchandise arrive at the toll-gate, four or five collectors shall take down who the merchants are, whence they come, what amount of merchandise they have brought and where for the first time the sealmark (*abhijnánamudrá*) has been made (on the merchandise).

Those whose merchandise has not been stamped with sealmark shall pay twice the amount of toll. For counterfeit seal they shall pay eight times the toll. If the sealmark is effaced or torn, (the merchants in question) shall be compelled to stand in *ghatikásthána*. When one kind of seal is used for another or when one kind of merchandise has been otherwise named (*námakrite*), the merchants shall pay a fine of 1¼ *panás* for each load (*sapádapanikam vahanam dápayet*).

The merchandise being placed near the flag of the toll-house, the merchants shall declare its quantity and price, cry out thrice "who will purchase this quantity of merchandise for this amount of price," and hand over the same to those who demand it (for that price). When purchasers happen to bid for it, the enhanced amount of the price together with the toll on the merchandise shall be paid into the king's treasury. When under the fear of having to pay a heavy toll, the quantity or the price of merchandise is lowered, the excess shall be taken by the king or the merchants shall be made to pay eight times the toll. The same punishment shall be imposed when the price of the merchandise packed in bags is lowered by showing an inferior sort as its sample or when valuable merchandise is covered over with a layer of an inferior one.

When under the fear of bidders (enhancing the price), the price of any merchandise is increased beyond its proper value, the king shall receive the enhanced amount or twice the amount of toll on it. The same punishment or eight times the amount of toll shall be imposed on the Superintendent of tolls if he conceals (merchandise).

Hence commodities shall be sold only after they are precisely weighed, measured, or numbered.

With regard to inferior commodities as well as those which are to be let off free of toll, the amount of toll due shall be determined after careful consideration.

Those merchants who pass beyond the flag of the toll-house without paying the toll shall be fined eight times the amount of the toll due from them.

Those who pass by to and from (the city) shall ascertain (whether or not toll has been paid on any merchandise going along the road.)

Commodities intended for marriages, or taken by a bride from her parents' house to her husband's (*anváyanam*), or intended for presentation, or taken for the purpose of sacrificial performance, confinement of women, worship of gods, ceremony of tonsure, investiture of sacred thread, gift of cows (*godána*, made before marriage), any religious rite, consecration ceremony (*dikshá*), and other special ceremonials shall be let off free of toll.

Those who utter a lie shall be punished as thieves.

Those who smuggle a part of merchandise on which toll has not been paid with that on which toll has been paid as well as those who, with a view to smuggle with one pass a second portion of merchandise, put it along with the stamped merchandise after breaking open the bag shall forfeit the smuggled quantity and pay as much fine as is equal to the quantity so smuggled.

He who, falsely swearing by cowdung, smuggles merchandise, shall be punished with the highest amercement.

When a person imports such forbidden articles as weapons (*sastra*), mail armour, metals, chariots, precious stones, grains and cattle, he shall not only be punished as laid down elsewhere, but also be made to forfeit his merchandise. When any of such commodities has been brought in for sale, they shall be sold, free of toll far outside (the fort).

The officer in charge of boundaries (*antapála*) shall receive a *pana*-and-a-quarter as roadcess (*vartani*) on each load of merchandise (*panyavahanasya*).

He shall levy a *pana* on a single-hoofed animal, half a *pana* on each head of cattle, and a quarter on a minor quadruped.

He shall also receive a *másha* on a head-load of merchandise.

He shall also make good whatever has been lost by merchants (in the part of the country under his charge).

After carefully examining foreign commodities as to their superior or inferior quality and stamping them with his seal, he shall send the same to the superintendent of tolls.

Or he may send to the king a spy in the guise of a trader with information as to the quantity and quality of the merchandise. (Having received this information,) the king shall in turn send it to the superintendent of tolls in view of exhibiting the king's omniscient power. The superintendent shall tell the merchants (in question) that such and such a merchant has brought such and such amount of superior or inferior merchandise, which none can possibly hide, and that that information is due to the omniscient power of the king.

For hiding inferior commodities, eight times the amount of toll shall be imposed; and for hiding or concealing superior commodities, they shall be wholly confiscated.

Whatever causes harm or is useless to the country shall be shut out; and whatever is of immense good as well as seeds not easily available shall be let in free of toll.

XXII. REGULATION OF TOLL-DUES.

MERCHANDISE, external (*báhyam, i.e.,* arriving from country parts), internal (*ábhyantaram, i.e.,* manufactured inside forts), or foreign (*átithyani, i.e.,* imported from foreign countries) shall all be liable to the payment of toll alike when exported (*nishkrámya*) and imported (*pravésyam*).

Imported commodities shall pay 1/5th of their value as toll.

Of flower, fruit, vegetables (*sáka*), roots (*múla*), bulbous roots (*kanda*), *pallikya* (?), seeds, dried fish, and dried meat, the superintendent shall receive 1/6th as toll.

As regards conch-shells, diamonds, precious stones, pearls, corals, and necklaces, experts acquainted with the time, cost, and finish of the production of such articles shall fix the amount of toll.

Of fibrous garments (*kshauma*), cotton cloths (*dukúla*), silk (*krimitána*), mail armour (*kankata*), sulphuret of arsenic (*haritála*), red arsenic (*manassilá*), vermilion (*hingulaka*), metals (*lóha*), and colouring ingredients (*varnadhátu*); of sandal, brown sandal (*agaru*), pungents (*katuka*), ferments (*kinva*), dress (*ávarana*), and the like; of wine, ivory, skins, raw materials used in making fibrous or cotton garments, carpets, curtains (*právarana*), and products yielded by worms (*krimijáta*); and of wool and other products yielded by goats and sheep, he shall receive 1/10th or 1/15th as toll.

Of cloths (*vastra*), quadrupeds, bipeds, threads, cotton, scents, medicines, wood, bamboo, fibres (*valkala*), skins, and clay-pots; of grains, oils, sugar (*kshára*), salt, liquor (*madya*) cooked rice and the like, he shall receive 1/20th or 1/25th as toll.

Gate-dues (*dvárádeya*) shall be 1/5th of toll dues; this tax may be remitted if circumstances necessitate such favour. Commodities shall never be sold where they are grown or manufactured.

When minerals and other commodities are purchased from mines, a fine of 600 *panás* shall be imposed.

When flower or fruits are purchased from flower or fruit gardens, a fine of 54 *panas* shall be imposed.

When vegetables, roots, bulbous roots are purchased from vegetable gardens, a fine 51¾ *panas* shall be imposed.

When any kind of grass or grain is purchased from field, a fine of 53 *panas* shall be imposed.

(Permanent) fines of 1 *pana* and 1½ *panas* shall be levied on agricultural produce (*sítátyayah*).

Hence in accordance with the customs of countries or of communities, the rate of toll shall be fixed on commodities, either old or new; and fines shall be fixed in proportion to the gravity of offences.

XXIII. SUPERINTENDENT OF WEAVING.

THE Superintendent of Weaving shall employ qualified persons to manufacture threads (*sútra*), coats (*varma*), cloths (*vastra*), and ropes.

Widows, cripple women, girls, mendicant or ascetic women (*pravrajitá*), women compelled to work in default of paying fines (*dandápratikáriní*), mothers of prostitutes, old women-servants of the king, and prostitutes (*devadási*) who have ceased to attend temples on service shall be employed to cut wool, fibre, cotton, panicle (*túla*), hemp, and flax.

Wages shall be fixed according as the threads spun are fine, coarse (*sthúla, i.e.*, big) or of middle quality and in proportion to a greater or less quantity manufactured, and in consideration of the quantity of thread spun, those (who turn out a greater quantity) shall be presented with oil and dried cakes of *myrobalan* fruits (*tailámalakódvartanaih*).

They may also be made to work on holidays (*tithishu*) by payment of special rewards (*prativápadánamánaih*).

Wages shall be cut short, if making allowance for the quality of raw material, the quantity of the threads spun out is found to fall short.

Weaving may also be done by those artisans who are qualified to turn out a given amount of work in a given time and for a fixed amount of wages.

The superintendent shall closely associate with the workmen.

Those who manufacture fibrous cloths, raiments, silk-cloths, woollen cloths, and cotton fabrics shall be rewarded by presentations such as scents, garlands of flowers, or any other prizes of encouragement.

Various kinds of garments, blankets, and curtains shall be manufactured.

Those who are acquainted with the work shall manufacture mail armour.

Those women who do not stir out of their houses (*anishkásinyah*), those whose husbands are gone abroad, and those who are cripple or girls may, when obliged to work for subsistence, be provided with work (spinning out threads) in due courtesy through the medium of maid-servants (of the weaving establishment.)

Those women who can present themselves at the weaving house shall at dawn be enabled to exchange their spinnings for wages (*bhándavetanavinimayam*). Only so much light as is enough to examine the threads shall be kept. If the superintendent looks at the face of such women or talks about any other work, he shall be punished with the first amercement. Delay in paying the wages shall be punished with the middlemost amercement. Likewise when wages are paid for work that is not completed.

She who, having received wages, does not turn out the work shall have her thumb cut off.

Those who misappropriate, steal, or run away with, (the raw material supplied to them) shall be similarly punished.

Weavers, when guilty, shall be fined out of their wages in proportion to their offences.

The superintendent shall closely associate with those who manufacture ropes and mail armour and shall carry on the manufacture of straps (*varatra*) and other commodities.

He shall carry on the manufacture of ropes from threads and fibres and of straps from cane and bamboo bark, with which beasts for draught are trained or tethered.

XXIV. THE SUPERINTENDENT OF AGRICULTURE.

POSSESSED of the knowledge of the science of agriculture dealing with the plantation of bushes and trees (*krishitantragulmavrikshsháyurvedajñah*), or assisted by those who are trained in such sciences, the superintendent of agriculture shall in time collect the seeds of all kinds of grains, flowers, fruits, vegetables, bulbous roots, roots, *pállikya* (?), fibre-producing plants, and cotton.

He shall employ slaves, labourers, and prisoners (*dandapratikartri*) to sow the seeds on crown-lands which have been often and satisfactorily ploughed.

The work of the above men shall not suffer on account of any want in ploughs (*karshanayantra*) and other necessary instruments or of bullocks. Nor shall there be any delay in procuring to them the assistence of blacksmiths, carpenters, borers (*medaka*), ropemakers, as well as those who catch snakes, and similar persons.

Any loss due to the above persons shall be punished with a fine equal to the loss.

The quantity of rain that falls in the country of *jángala* is 16 *dronas*; half as much more in moist countries (*anúpánám*); as to the countries which are fit for agriculture (*désavápánam*);-- 13½ *dronas* in the country of *asmakas*; 23 *dronas* in*avantí*; and an immense quantity in western countries (*aparántánám*), the borders of the Himalayas, and the countries where water channels are made use of in agriculture (*kulyávápánám*).

When one-third of the requisite quantity of rain falls both during the commencement and closing months of the rainy season and two-thirds in the middle, then the rainfall is (considered) very even (*sushumárúpam*).

A forecast of such rainfall can be made by observing the position, motion, and pregnancy (*garbhádána*) of the Jupiter

(*Brihaspati*), the rise and set and motion of the Venus, and the natural or unnatural aspect of the sun.

From the sun, the sprouting of the seeds can be inferred; from (the position of) the Jupiter, the formation of grains (*stambakarita*) can be inferred; and from the movements of the Venus, rainfall can be inferred.

Three are the clouds that continuously rain for seven days; eighty are they that pour minute drops; and sixty are they that appear with the sunshine--this is termed rainfall. Where rain, free from wind and unmingled with sunshine, falls so as to render three turns of ploughing possible, there the reaping of good harvest is certain.

Hence, *i.e.*, according as the rainfall is more or less, the superintendent shall sow the seeds which require either more or less water.

Sáli (a kind of rice), *vríhi* (rice), *kodrava* (Paspalum Scrobiculatum), *tila* (sesamum), *priyangu* (panic seeds), *dáraka* (?), and *varaka* (Phraseolus Trilobus) are to be sown at the commencement (*púrvávápah*) of the rainy season.

Mudga (Phraseolus Mungo), *másha* (Phraseolus Radiatus), and *saibya* (?) are to be sown in the middle of the season.

Kusumbha (safflower), *masúra* (Ervum Hirsutum), *kuluttha* (Dolichos Uniflorus), *yava* (barley), *godhúma* (wheat), *kaláya* (leguminus seeds), *atasi* (linseed), and *sarshapa* (mustard) are to be sown last.

Or seeds may be sown according to the changes of the season.

Fields that are left unsown (*vápátiriktam*, *i.e.*, owing to the inadequacy of hands) may be brought under cultivation by employing those who cultivate for half the share in the produce (*ardhasítiká*); or those who live by their own physical exertion (*svavíryopajívinah*) may cultivate such fields for ¼th or 1/5th of the produce grown; or they may pay (to the king) as much as they can without entailing any hardship upon themselves (*anavasitam bhágam*), with the exception of their own private lands that are difficult to cultivate.

Those who cultivate irrigating by manual labour (*hastaprávartimam*) shall pay 1/5th of the produce as water-rate (*udakabhágam*); by carrying water on shoulders (*skandhaprávartimam*) ¼th of the produce; by water-lifts (*srotoyantraprávartimam*), ⅓rd of the produce; and by raising water from rivers, lakes, tanks, and wells (*nadisarastatákakúpodghátam*),⅓rd or ¼th of the produce.

The superintendent shall grow wet crops (*kedára*), winter-crops (*haimana*), or summer crops (*graishmika*) according to the supply of workmen and water.

Rice-crops and the like are the best (*jyáshtha, i.e.*, to grow); vegetables (*shanda*) are of intermediate nature; and sugarcane crops (*ikshu*) are the worst (*pratyavarah, i.e.*, very difficult to grow), for they are subject to various evils and require much care and expenditure to reap.

Lands that are beaten by foam (*phenághátah, i.e.*, banks of rivers, etc.) are suitable for growing *vallíphala* (pumpkin, gourd and the like); lands that are frequently overflown by water (*parívháhánta*) for long pepper, grapes (*mridvíká*), and sugarcane; the vicinity of wells for vegetables and roots; low grounds (*hariníparyantáh*) for green crops; and marginal furrows between any two rows of crops are suitable for the plantation of fragrant plants, medicinal herbs, cascus roots (*usínara*), *híra* (?), *beraka* (?), and *pindáluka* (lac) and the like.

Such medicinal herbs as grow in marshy grounds are to be grown not only in grounds suitable for them, but also in pots (sthályam).

The seeds of grains are to be exposed to mist and heat (*tushárapáyanamushnam cha*) for seven nights; the seeds of *kosi* are treated similarly for three nights; the seeds of sugarcane and the like (*kándabíjánam*) are plastered at the cut end with the mixture of honey, clarified butter, the fat of hogs, and cowdung; the seeds of bulbous roots (*kanda*) with honey and clarified butter; cotton seeds (*asthibíja*) with cow-dung; and water pits at the root of trees are to be burnt and manured with the bones and dung of cows on proper occasions.

The sprouts of seeds, when grown, are to be manured with a fresh haul of minute fishes and irrigated with the milk of *snuhi* (Euphorbia Antiquorum).

Where there is the smoke caused by burning the essence of cotton seeds and the slough of a snake, there snakes will not stay.

Always while sowing seeds, a handful of seeds bathed in water with a piece of gold shall be sown first and the following mantra recited:--

"Prajápatye Kasyapáya déváya namah. Sadá Sítá medhyatám déví bíjéshu cha dhanéshu cha. Chandaváta hé."

"Salutation to God *Prajápati Kasyapa*. Agriculture may always flourish and the Goddess (may reside) in seeds and wealth. *Channdavata he*."

Provisions shall be supplied to watchmen, slaves and labourers in proportion to the amount of work done by them.

They shall be paid a *pana*-and-a-quarter per *mensem*. Artisans shall be provided with wages and provision in proportion to the amount of work done by them.

Those that are learned in the Vedas and those that are engaged in making penance may take from the fields ripe flowers and fruits for the purpose of worshipping their gods, and rice and barley for the purpose of performing ágrayana, a sacrificial performance at the commencement of harvest season, also those who live by gleaning grains in fields may gather grains where grains had been accumulated and removed from.

Grains and other crops shall be collected as often as they are harvested. No wise man shall leave anything in the fields, nor even chaff. Crops, when reaped, shall be heaped up in high piles or in the form of turrets. The piles of crops shall not be kept close, nor shall their tops be small or low. The threshing floors of different fields shall be situated close to each other. Workmen in the fields shall always have water but no fire.

XXV. THE SUPERINTENDENT OF LIQUOR.

BY employing such men as are acquainted with the manufacture of liquor and ferments (*kinva*), the Superintendent of Liquor shall carry on liquor-traffic not only in forts and country parts, but also in camps.

In accordance with the requirements of demand and supply (*krayavikrayavasena*) he may either centralize or decentralize the sale of liquor.

A fine of 600 *panas* shall be imposed on all offenders other than those who are manufacturers, purchasers, or sellers in liquor-traffic.

Liquor shall not be taken out of villages, nor shall liquor shops be close to each other.

Lest workmen spoil the work in hand, and *Aryas* violate their decency and virtuous character, and lest firebrands commit indiscreet acts, liquor shall be sold to persons of well known character in such small quantities as one-fourth or half-a-*kudumba*, one *kudumba*, half-a-*prastha*, or one *prastha*. Those who are well known and of pure character may take liquor out of shop.

Or all may be compelled to drink liquor within the shops and not allowed to stir out at once in view of detecting articles such as sealed deposits, unsealed deposits, commodities given for repair, stolen articles, and the like which the customer's may have acquired by foul means. When they are found to possess gold and other articles not their own, the superintendent shall contrive to cause them to be arrested outside the shop. Likewise those who are too extravagant or spend beyond their income shall be arrested.

No fresh liquor other than bad liquor shall be sold below its price. Bad liquor may be sold elsewhere or given to slaves or workmen in lieu of wages; or it may form the drink of beasts for draught or the subsistence of hogs.

Liquor shops shall contain many rooms provided with beds and seats kept apart. The drinking room shall contain scents, garlands of flowers, water, and other comfortable things suitable to the varying seasons.

Spies stationed in the shops shall ascertain whether the expenditure incurred by customers in the shop is ordinary or extraordinary and also whether there are any strangers. They shall also ascertain the value of the dress, ornaments, and gold of the customers lying there under intoxication.

When customers under intoxication lose any of their things, the merchants of the shop shall not only make good the loss, but also pay an equivalent fine.

Merchants seated in half-closed rooms shall observe the appearance of local and foreign customers who, in real or false guise of *Aryas* lie down in intoxication along with their beautiful mistresses.

Of various kinds of liquor such as *medaka*, *prasanna*, *ásava*, *arista*, *maireya*, and *madhu*:--

Medaka is manufactured with one *drona* of water, half, an *ádaka* of rice, and three *prastha* of *kinva* (ferment).

Twelve *ádhakas* of flour (*pishta*), five *prasthas* of *kinva* (ferment), with the addition of spices (*játisambhára*) together with the bark and fruits of *putraká* (a species of tree) constitute *prasanná*.

One-hundred *palas* of *kapittha* (Feronia Elephantum) 500 *palas* of *phánita* (sugar), and one *prastha* of honey (*madhu*) form *ásava*.

With an increase of one-quarter of the above ingredients, a superior kind of *ásava* is manufactured; and when the same ingredients are lessened to the extent of one-quarter each, it becomes of an inferior quality.

The preparation of various kinds of *arishta* for various diseases are to be learnt from physicians.

A sour gruel or decoction of the bark of *meshasringi* (a kind of poison) mixed with *jaggery* (*guda*) and with the powder of long pepper and black pepper or with the powder of *triphala* (1

Terminalia Chebula, 2 Terminalia Bellerica, and 3 Phyllanthus Emblica) forms *Maireya*.

To all kinds of liquor mixed with *jaggery*, the powder of *triphala* is always added.

The juice of grapes is termed *madhu*. Its own native place (*svadesa*) is the commentary on such of its various forms as *kápisáyana* and *hárahúraka*.

One *drona* of either boiled or unboiled paste of *másha* (Phraseolus Radiatus), three parts more of rice, and one *karsha* of *morata* (Alangium Hexapetalum) and the like form *kinva* (ferment).

In the manufacture of *medaka* and *prasanna*, five *karshas* of the powder of (each of *páthá* (Clypea Hermandifolio), *lodhra* (Symplocos Racemosa), *tejovati* (Piper Chaba), *eláváluka* (Solanum Melongena) honey, the juice of grapes (*madhurasa*), *priyangu* (panic seeds), *dáruharidra* (a species of turmeric) black pepper and long pepper are added as *sambhára*, requisite spices.

The decoction of *madhúka* (Bassia Latifolia) mixed with granulated sugar (*katasarkará*), when added to *prasanna*, gives it a pleasing colour.

The requisite quantity of spices to be added to *ásava* is one *karshá* of the powder of each of *chocha* (bark of cinnamon), *chitraka* (Plumbago Zeylanica), *vilanga*, and *gajapippalí* (Scindapsus Officinalis), and two *karshas* of the powder of each of *kramuka* (betel nut), *madhúka* (Bassia Latifolia), *mustá* (Cyprus Rotundus), and *lodhra* (Symlocos Racemosa).

The addition of one-tenth of the above ingredients (*i.e.*, *chocha*, *kramuka*, etc.), is (termed) *bíjabandha*.

The same ingredients as are added to *prasanná* are also added to white liquor (*svetasurá*).

The liquor that is manufactured from mango fruits (*sahakárasurá*) may contain a greater proportion of mango essence (*rasottara*), or of spices (*bíjottara*). It is called *mahásura* when it contains *sambhára* (spices as described above).

When a handful (*antarnakho mushtih, i.e.*, so much as can be held in the hand, the fingers being so bent that the nails cannot be seen) of the powder of granulated sugar dissolved in the decoction of *moratá* (Alangium Hexapetalum), *palása*(Butea Frondosa), *dattúra* (Dattura Fastuosa), *karanja* (Robinia Mitis), *meshasringa* (a kind of poison) and the bark of milky trees (*kshiravriksha*) mixed with one-half of the paste formed by combining the powders of *lodhra* (Symplocos Racemosa), *chitraka* (Plumbago Zeylanica), *vilanga*, *páthá* (clypea Hermandifolia), *mustá* (cyprus Rotundus), *kaláya* (leguminous seeds), *dáruharidra* (Amonum Xanthorrhizon), *indívara* (blue lotus), *satapushpa* (Anethum Sowa), *apámárga*(Achyranthes Aspera) *saptaparna* (Echites Scholaris), and *nimba* (Nimba Melia) is added to (even) a *kumbha* of liquor payable by the king, it renders it very pleasant. Five *palas* of *phánita* (sugar) are added to the above in order to increase its flavour.

On special occasions (*krityeshu*), people (*kutumbinah, i.e.*, families) shall be allowed to manufacture white liquor (*svetasura*), *arishta* for use in diseases, and other kinds of liquor.

On the occasions of festivals, fairs (*samája*), and pilgrimage, right of manufacture of liquor for four days (*chaturahassaurikah*) shall be allowed.

The Superintendent shall collect the daily fines (*daivasikamatyayam, i.e.*, license fees) from those who on these occasions are permitted to manufacture liquor.

Women and children shall collect '*sura*,' and '*kinva*,' 'ferment.'

Those who deal with liquor other than that of the king shall pay five percent as toll.

With regard to *sura*, *medaka*, *arishta*, wine, *phalámla* (acid drinks prepared from fruits), and *ámlasídhu* (spirit distilled from molasses):--

Having ascertained the day's sale of the above kinds of liquor, the difference of royal and public measures (*mánavyáji*), and the excessive amount of sale proceeds realised thereby, the Superintendent shall fix the amount of compensation (*vaidharana*) due to the king (from local or foreign merchants for entailing loss on the king's liquor traffic) and shall always adopt the best course.

XXVI. THE SUPERINTENDENT OF SLAUGHTER-HOUSE.

WHEN a person entraps, kills, or molests deer, bison, birds, and fish which are declared to be under State protection or which live in forests under State-protection (*abhayáranya*), he shall be punished with the highest amercement.

Householders trespassing in forest preserves shall be punished with the middlemost amercement.

When a person entraps, kills, or molests either fish or birds that do not prey upon other animals, he shall be fined 26¾ *panas*; and when he does the same to deer and other beasts, he shall be fined twice as much.

Of beasts of prey that have been captured, the Superintendent shall take one-sixth; of fish and birds (of similar nature), he shall take one-tenth or more than one-tenth; and of deer and other beasts (*mrigapasu*), one-tenth or more than one-tenth as toll.

One-sixth of live animals such as birds and beasts shall be let off in forests under State-protection.

Elephants, horses or animals having the form of a man, bull or an ass living in oceans as well as fish in tanks, lakes, channels and rivers; and such game-birds as *krauncha* (a kind of heron), *utkrosaka* (osprey), *dátyúha* (a sort of cuckoo),*hamsa* (flamingo), *chakraváka* (a brahmany duck), *jivanjívaka* (a kind of pheasant), *bhringarája* (*Lanius Malabaricus*), *chakora* (partridge), *m attakokila* (cuckoo), peacock, parrot, and maina (*madanasárika*) as well as other auspicious animals, whether birds or beasts, shall be protected from all kinds of molestations.

Those who violate the above rule shall be punished with the first amercement.

(Butchers) shall sell fresh and boneless flesh of beasts (*mrigapasu*) just killed.

If they sell bony flesh, they shall give an equivalent compensation (*pratipákam*).

If there is any diminution in weight owing to the use of a false balance, they shall give eight times the diminution.

Cattle such as a calf, a bull, or a milch cow shall not be slaughtered.

He who slaughters or tortures them to death shall be fined 50 *panas*.

The flesh of animals which have been killed outside the slaughter-house (*parisúnam*), headless, legless and boneless flesh, rotten flesh, and the flesh of animals which have suddenly died shall not be sold. Otherwise a fine of 12 *panas* shall be imposed.

Cattle, wild beasts, elephants (*vyala*), and fish living in forests under State protection shall, if they become of vicious nature, be entrapped and killed outside the forest preserve.

XXVII. THE SUPERINTENDENT OF PROSTITUTES.

THE Superintendent of Prostitutes shall employ (at the king's court) on a salary of 1,000 *panas* (per annum) a prostitute (*ganiká*), whether born or not born of a prostitute's family, and noted for her beauty, youth, and accomplishments.

A rival prostitute (*pratiganiká*) on half the above salary (kutumbárdhéna) shall also be appointed.

Whenever such a prostitute goes abroad or dies, her daughter or sister shall act for her and receive her property and salary. Or her mother may substitute another prostitute. In the absence of any of these, the king himself shall take the property.

With a view to add to the splendour of prostitutes holding the royal umbrella, golden pitcher, and fan, and attending upon the king seated on his royal litter, throne, or chariot, prostitutes shall be classified as of first, middle and highest rank according to their beauty and splendid jewellery; likewise their salary shall be fixed by thousands.

She who has lost her beauty shall be appointed as a nurse (*mátriká*).

A prostitute shall pay 24,000 *panas* as ransom to regain her liberty; and a prostitute's son 12,000 *panas*.

From the age of eight years, a prostitute shall hold musical performance before the king.

Those prostitutes, female slaves, and old women who are incapable of rendering any service in the form of enjoyment (*bhagnabhogáh*) shall work in the storehouse or kitchen of the king.

A prostitute who, putting herself under the protection of a private person, ceases to attend the king's court shall pay a *pana*-and-a-quarter per *mensem* (to the Government).

The superintendent shall determine the earnings, inheritance, income (*áya*), expenditure, and future earnings (*áyati*) of every prostitute.

He shall also check their extravagant expenditure.

When a prostitute puts her jewellery in the hands of any person but her mother, she shall be fined 4¼ *panas*.

If she sells or mortgages her property (*svapateyam*), she shall be fined 50¼ *panas*.

A prostitute shall be fined 24 *panas* for defamation; twice as much for causing hurt; and 50¼ *panas* as well as 1½ *panas* for cutting off the ear (of any person).

When a man has connection with a prostitute against her will or with a prostitute girl (*kumári*), he shall be punished with the highest amercement. But when he has connection with a willing prostitute, (under age), he shall be punished with the first amercement.

When a man keeps under confinement, or abducts, a prostitute against her will, or disfigures her by causing hurt, he shall be fined 1,000 *panas* or more rising up to twice the amount of her ransom (*nishkraya*) according to the circumstances of the crime and the position and the status of the prostitute (*sthánaviseshena*).

When a man causes hurt to a prostitute appointed at the court (*praptádhikáram*), he shall be fined thrice the amount of her ransom.

When a man causes hurt to a prostitute's mother, to her young daughter, or to a *rúpadási*, he shall be punished with the highest amercement.

In all cases of offences, punishment for offences committed for the first time shall be the first amercement; twice as much for offences committed for a second time; thrice as much for the third time; and for offences committed for the fourth time, the king may impose any punishment he likes.

When a prostitute does not yield her person to any one under the orders of the king, she shall receive 1000 lashes with a whip or pay a fine of 5,000 *panas*.

When having received the requisite amount of fees, a prostitute dislikes to yield her person, she shall be fined twice the amount of the fees.

When, in her own house, a prostitute deprives her paramour of his enjoyment, she shall be fined eight times the amount of the fees unless the paramour happens to be unassociable on account of disease and personal defects.

When a prostitute murders her paramour, she shall be burnt alive or thrown into water.

When a paramour steals the jewellery or money of, or deceives to pay the fees due to, a prostitute, he shall be fined eight times that amount.

Every prostitute shall supply information to the superintendent as to the amount of her daily fees (*bhoga*), her future income (*úyuli*), and the paramour (under her influence).

The same rules shall apply to an actor, dancer, singer, player on musical instruments, a buffoon (*vágjivana*), a mimic player (*kusílava*), rope-dancer (*plavaka*), a juggler (*saubhika*), a wandering bard or herald (*chárana*), pimps, and unchaste women.

When persons of the above description come from foreign countries to hold their performances, they shall pay 5 *panas* as license fee (*prekshávetana*).

Every prostitute (*rúpájivá*) shall pay every month twice the amount of a day's earning (*bhogadvigunam*) to the Government.

Those who teach prostitutes, female slaves, and actresses, arts such as singing, playing on musical instruments, reading, dancing, acting, writing, painting, playing on the instruments like *vina*, pipe, and drum, reading the thoughts of others, manufacture of scents and garlands, shampooing, and the art of attracting and captivating the mind of others shall be endowed with maintenance from the State.

They (the teachers) shall train the sons of prostitutes to be chief actors (*rangopajívi*) on the stage.

The wives of actors and others of similar profession who have been taught various languages and the use of signals (*sanja*) shall, along with their relatives, be made use of in detecting the wicked and murdering or deluding foreign spies.

XXVIII. THE SUPERINTENDENT OF SHIPS.

THE Superintendent of Ships shall examine the accounts relating to navigation not only on oceans and mouths of rivers, but also on lakes natural or artificial, and rivers in the vicinity of *stháníya* and other fortified cities.

Villages on seashores or on the banks of rivers and lakes shall pay a fixed amount of tax (*kliptam*).

Fishermen shall give 1/6th of their haul as fees for fishing license (*naukáhátakam*).

Merchants shall pay the customary toll levied in port-towns.

Passengers arriving on board the king's ship shall pay the requisite amount of sailing fees (*yátrávetanam*).

Those (who make use of the king's boats in) fishing out conch-shells and pearls shall pay the requisite amount of hire (*Naukáhátakam*), or they may make use of their own boats.

The duties of the superintendent of mines will explain those of the superintendent of conch-shells and pearls.

The superintendent of ships shall strictly observe the customs prevalent in commercial towns as well as the orders of the superintendent of towns (*pattana*, port town).

Whenever a weatherbeaten ship arrives at a port-town, he shall show fatherly kindness to it.

Vessels carrying on merchandise spoiled by water may either be exempted from toll or may have their toll reduced to half and let to sail when the time for setting sail approaches.

Ships that touch at harbours on their way may be requested the payment of toll.

Pirate ships (*himsríká*), vessels which are bound for the country of an enemy, as well as those which have violated the customs and rules in force in port towns shall be destroyed.

In those large rivers which cannot be forded even during the winter and summer seasons, there shall be launched large boats (*mahánávah*) provided with a captain (*sásaka*), a steersman (*niyámaka*), and servants to hold the sickle and the ropes and to pour out water.

Small boats shall be launched in those small rivers which overflow during the rainy season.

Fording or crossing the rivers (without permission) shall be prohibited lest traitors may cross them (and escape).

When a person fords or crosses a river outside the proper place and in unusual times, he shall be punished with the first amercement.

When a man fords or crosses a river at the usual place and time without permission, he shall be fined 26¾ *panas*.

Fishermen, carriers of firewood, grass, flowers, and fruits, gardeners, vegetable-dealers, and herdsmen, persons pursuing suspected criminals, messengers following other messengers going in advance, servants engaged to carry things, provisions, and orders to the army, those who use their own ferries, as well as those who supply villages of marshy districts with seeds, necessaries of life, commodities and other accessary things shall be exempted (to cross rivers at any time and place).

Bráhmans, ascetics (*pravrajita*), children, the aged, the afflicted, royal messengers, and pregnant women shall be provided by the superintendent with free passes to cross rivers.

Foreign merchants who have often been visiting the country as well as those who are well known to local merchants shall be allowed to land in port-towns.

Any person who is abducting the wife or daughter of another, one who is carrying off the wealth of another, a suspected person, one who seems to be of perturbed appearance, one who has no baggage, one who attempts to conceal, or evade the cognisance of the valuable load in one's hand, one who has just put on a different garb, one who has removed or renounced one's usual garb, one who has just turned out an ascetic, one who pretends to be suffering from disease, one who seems to be alarmed, one who is stealthily carrying valuable things, or going on a secret mission, or carrying weapons or explosives (*agniyoga*), one who holds poison in one's hand, and one who has come from a long distance without a pass shall all be arrested.

A minor quadruped as well as a man carrying some load shall pay one *másha*.

A head-load, a load carried on shoulders (*káyabhárah*), a cow, and a horse shall each pay 2 *máshas*.

A camel and a buffalo shall each pay 4 *máshas*.

A small cart (*laghuyána*) 5 *máshas*; and a cart (of medium size) drawn by bulls (*golingam*) shall pay 6 *máshas* and a big cart (*sakata*) 7 *máshas*.

A head-load of merchandise ¼ *másha*; this explains other kinds of loads. In big rivers, ferry-fees are double the above. Villages near marshy places shall give (to the ferry-men) the prescribed amount of food-stuff and wages.

In boundaries, ferry-men shall receive the toll, carriage-cess, and road-cess. They shall also confiscate the property of the person travelling without a pass. The Superintendent of Boats shall make good the loss caused by the loss of the boat due to the heavy load, sailing in improper time or place, want of ferry-men, or lack of repair. Boats should be launched between the months of *Ashádha*, the first seven days being omitted, and *Kártika*; the evidence of a ferryman should be given and the daily income should be remitted.

XXIX. THE SUPERINTENDENT OF COWS.

THE Superintendent of cows shall supervise (1) herds maintained for wages (*vétanópagráhikam*), (2) herds surrendered for a fixed amount of dairy produce (*karapratikara*), (3) useless and abandoned herds (*bhagnotsrishtakam*), (4) herds maintained for a share in dairy produce (*bhágánupravishtam*), (5) classes of herds (*vrajaparyagram*), (6) cattle that strayed (*nashtam*), (7) cattle that are irrecoverably lost (*vinashtam*), and (8) the amassed quantity of milk and clarified butter.

(1) When a cowherd, a buffalo-herdsman, a milker, a churner, and a hunter (*lubdhaka*) fed by wages graze milch cows (*dhenu*) in hundreds (*satam satam*)--for if they graze the herds for the profit of milk and *ghi*, they will starve the calves to death,--that system of rearing the cattle is termed 'herds maintained for wages.'

(2) When a single person rears a hundred heads (*rúpasatam*) made up of equal numbers of each of aged cows, milch cows, pregnant cows, heifers, and calves (*vatsatari*) and gives (to the owner) 8 *várakas* of clarified butter per annum, as well as the branded skin (of dead cows if any), that system is called 'herds surrendered for a fixed amount of dairy produce.'

(3) When those who rear a hundred heads made up of equal numbers of each of afflicted cattle, crippled cattle, cattle that

cannot be milked by any one but the accustomed person, cattle that are not easily milked, and cattle that kill their own calves give in return (to the owner) a share in dairy produce, it is termed 'useless and abandoned herd.'

(4) When under the fear of cattle-lifting enemies (*parachakrátavibhayát*), cattle are kept under the care of the superintendent, giving him 1/10th of the dairy produce for his protection, it is termed "herds maintained for a share in dairy produce."

(5) When the superintendent classifies cattle as calves, steers, tameable ones, draught oxen, bulls that are to be trained to yoke, bulls kept for crossing cows, cattle that are fit only for the supply of flesh, buffaloes and draught buffaloes; female calves, female steer, heifer, pregnant cows, milch cattle, barren cattle---either cows or buffaloes; calves that are a month or two old as well as those which are still younger; and when, as he ought to, he brands them all inclusive of their calves of one or two months old along with those stray cattle which have remained unclaimed in the herds for a month or two; and when he registers the branded marks, natural marks, colour and the distance from one horn to another of each of the cattle, that system is known as 'class of herds.'

(6) When an animal is carried off by thieves or finds itself into the herds of others or strays unknown, it is called 'lost.'

(7) When an animal is entangled in a quagmire or precipice or dies of disease or of old age, or drowned in water: or when it is killed by the fall of a tree or of river bank, or is beaten to death with a staff or stone, or is struck by lightening (*ísána*), or is devoured by a tiger or bitten by a cobra, or is carried off by a crocodile, or is involved in the midst of a forest fire, it is termed as "irrecoverably lost."

Cowherds shall endeavour to keep them away from such dangers.

Whoever hurts or causes another to hurt, or steals or causes another to steal a cow, should be slain.

When a person substitutes an animal (*rúpa*) bearing the royal brand mark for a private one, he shall be punished with the first amercement.

When a person recovers a local cattle from thieves, he shall receive the promised reward (*panitam rúpam*); and when a man rescues a foreign cattle (from thieves), he shall receive half its value.

Cowherds shall apply remedies to calves or aged cows or cows suffering from diseases.

They shall graze the herds in forests which are severally allotted as pasture grounds for various seasons and from which thieves, tigers and other molesting beasts are driven away by hunters aided by their hounds.

With a view to scare out snakes and tigers and as a definite means of knowing the whereabouts of herds, sounding bells shall be attached to (the neck of) timid cattle.

Cowherds shall allow their cattle to enter into such rivers or lakes as are of equal depth all round, broad, and free from mire and crocodiles, and shall protect them from dangers under such circumstances.

Whenever an animal is caught hold of by a thief, a tiger, a snake, or a crocodile, or when it is too infirm owing to age or disease, they shall make a report of it; otherwise they shall be compelled to make good the loss.

When an animal dies a natural death, they shall surrender the skin with the brand mark, if it is a cow or a buffalo; the skin together with the ear (*karnalakshanam*) if it is a goat or sheep; the tail with the skin containing the brand mark, if it is an ass or a camel; the skin, if it is a young one; besides the above, (they shall also restore) the fat (*vasti*), bile, marrow (*snáyu*), teeth, hoofs, horns, and bones.

They (the cowherds) may sell either fresh flesh or dried flesh.

They shall give buttermilk as drink to dogs and hogs, and reserve a little (buttermilk) in a bronze vessel to prepare their own dish: they may also make use of coagulated milk or cheese (*kíláta*) to render their oilcakes relishing (*ghánapinyáka-kledartha*).

He who sells his cow (from among the herds) shall pay (to the king) ¼th *rúpa* (value of the cow).

During the rainy, autumnal, and the first part of winter (*hemanta*) seasons, they shall milk the cattle both the times (morning and evening); and during the latter part of winter and the whole of the spring and summer seasons, they shall milk only once (*i.e.*, only in the morning). The cowherd who milks a cow a second time during these seasons shall have his thumb cut off.

If he allows the time of milking to lapse, he shall forfeit the profit thereof (*i.e.*, the milk).

The same rule shall hold good in case of negligence of the opportune moment for putting a string through the nose of a bull and other animals, and for taming or training them to the yoke.

One *drona* of a cow's milk will, when churned, yield one *prastha* of butter; the same quantity of a buffalo's milk will yield 1/7th *prastha* more; and the same quantity of milk of goats and sheep will produce ½ *prastha* more.

In all kinds of milk, the exact quantity of butter shall be ascertained by churning; for increase in the supply of milk and butter depends on the nature of the soil and the quantity and quality of fodder and water.

When a person causes a bull attached to a herd to fight with another bull, he shall be punished with the first amercement; when a bull is injured (under such circumstances), he shall be punished with the highest amercement.

Cattle shall be grouped in herds of ten each of similar colour, while they are being grazed.

According to the protective strength of the cowherds the capacity of the cattle to go far and wide to graze, cowherds shall take their cattle either far or near.

Once in six months, sheep and other animals shall be shorn of their wool.

The same rules shall apply to herds of horses, asses, camels, and hogs.

For bulls which are provided with nose-rings, and which equal horses in speed and in carrying loads, half a *bhára* of meadow grass (*yavasa*), twice the above quantity of ordinary grass (*trina*), one *tulá* (100 *palas*) of oil cakes, 10 *ádhakas*of bran, 5 *palas* of salt (*mukhalavanam*), one *kudumba* of oil for rubbing over the nose (*nasya*), 1 *prastha* of drink (*pána*), one *tulá* of flesh, 1 *ádhaka* of *curis*, 1 *drona* of barley or of cooked *másha* (Phraseolus Radiatus), 1 *drona* of milk; or half an *ádhaka* of *surá* (liquor), 1 *prastha* of oil or *ghi* (*sneha*) 10 *palas* of sugar or jaggery, 1 *pala* of the fruit of *sringibera* (ginger) may be substituted for milk (*pratipána*).

The same commodities less by one quarter each will form the diet for mules, cows, and asses; twice the quantity of the above things for buffaloes and camels.

Draught oxen and cows, supplying milk (*payah*), shall be provided with subsistence in proportion to the duration of time the oxen are kept at work, and the quantity of milk which the cows supply.

All cattle shall be supplied with abundance of fodder and water.

Thus the manner of rearing herds of cattle has been dealt with.

A herd of 100 heads of asses and mules shall contain 5 male animals; that of goats and sheep ten; and a herd of ten heads of either cows or buffaloes shall contain four male animals.

XXX. THE SUPERINTENDENT OF HORSES.

THE Superintendent of Horses shall register the breed, age, colour, marks, group or classes, and the native place of horses, and classify as (1) those that are kept in sale-house for sale (*panyágárikam*), (2) those that are recently purchased (*krayopágatam*), (3) those that have been captured in wars (*áhavalabdham*), (4) those that are of local breed (*ájátam*), (5) those that are sent thither for help (*sáháyyakágatam*), (6) those that are mortgaged (*panasthitam*), and (7) those that are temporarily kept in stables (*yávatkálikam*).

He shall make a report (to the king) of such animals as are inauspicious, crippled, or diseased.

Every horseman shall know how to make an economic use of whatever he has received from the king's treasury and storehouse.

The superintendent shall have a stable constructed as spacious as required by the number of horses to be kept therein twice as broad as the length of a horse, with four doors facing the four quarters, with its central floor suited for the rolling of horses, with projected front provided with wooden seats at the entrance, and containing monkeys, peacocks, red spotted deer (*prishata*), mangoose, partridges (*chakora*), parrots, and maina birds (*sárika*); the room for every horse shall be four times as broad or long as the length of a horse, with its central floor paved with smoothened wooden planks, with separate compartments for fodder (*khádanakoshthakam*), with passages for the removal of urine and dung, and with a door facing either the north or the east. The distinction of quarters (*digvibhága*) may be made as a matter of fact or relatively to the situation of the building.

Steeds, stallions and colts shall be separately kept.

A steed that has just given birth to a colt shall be provided for the first three days with a drink of 1 *prastha* of clarified butter; afterwards it shall be fed with a *prastha* of flour (*saktu*) and made to drink oil mixed with medicine for ten nights; after that time, it shall have cooked grains, meadow grass, and other things suited to the season of the day.

A colt, ten days old, shall be given a *kudumba* of flour mixed with ¼th *kudumba* of clarified butter, and 1 *prastha* of milk till it becomes six months old; then the above rations shall be increased half as much during each succeeding month, with the addition of 1 *prastha* of barley till it becomes three years old, then one *drona* of barley till it grows four years old; at the age of four or five, it attains its full development and becomes serviceable.

The face (*mukha*) of the best horse measures 32 *angulas*; its length is 5 times its face; its shank is 20 *angulas*; and its height is 4 times its shank.

Horses of medium and lower sizes fall short of the above measurement by two and three *angulas* respectively.

The circumference (*parínáha*) of the best horse measures 100 *angulas*, and horses of medium and lower sizes fall short of the above measurement by five parts (*panchabhágávaram*).

For the best horse (the diet shall be) 2 *dronas* of any one of the grains, rice (*sáli, vríhi,*) barley, panic seeds (*priyangu*) soaked or cooked, cooked *mudga* (Phraseolus Munga) or *másha* (Phraseolus Radiatus); one *prastha* of oil, 5 *palas* of salt, 50 *palas* of flesh, 1 *ádhaka* of broth (rasa) or 2 *ádhakas* of curd, 5 *palas* of sugar (*kshára*), to make their diet relishing, 1 *prastha* of *súrá*, liquor, or 2 *prasthas* of milk.

The same quantity of drink shall be specially given to those horses which are tired of long journey or of carrying loads.

One *prastha* of oil for giving enema (*anuvásana*), 1 *kudumba* of oil for rubbing over the nose, 1,000 *palas* of meadow grass, twice as much of ordinary grass (*trina*); and hay-stalk or grass shall be spread over an area of 6 *aratnis*.

The same quantity of rations less by one-quarter for horses of medium and lower size.

A draught horse or stallion of medium size shall be given the same quantity as the best horse; and similar horses of lower size shall receive the same quantity as a horse of medium size.

Steeds and *párasamas* shall have one quarter less of rations.

Half of the rations given to steeds shall be given to colts.

Thus is the distribution of ration dealt with.

Those who cook the food of horses, grooms, and veterinary surgeons shall have a share in the rations (*pratisvadabhajah*).

Stallions which are incapacitated owing to old age, disease or hardships of war, and, being therefore rendered unfit for use in war live only to consume food shall in the interests of citizens and country people be allowed to cross steeds.

The breed of *Kámbhoja, Sindhu, Aratta,* and *Vanáyu* countries are the best; those of *Báhlíka, Pápeya, Sauvira,* and *Taitala*, are of middle quality; and the rest ordinary (*avaráh*).

These three sorts may be trained either for war or for riding according as they are furious (*tíkshna*), mild (*bhadra*), or stupid or slow (*manda*).

The regular training of a horse is its preparation for war (*sánnáhyam karma*).

Circular movement (*valgana*), slow movement (*níchairgata*), jumping (*langhana*), gallop (*dhorana*), and response to signals (*nároshtra*) are the several forms of riding (*aupaváhya*).

Aupavenuka, vardhmánaka, yamaka, álídhapluta, vrithatta and *trivacháli* are the varieties of circular movement (*valgana*).

The same kind of movements with the head and ear kept erect are called slow movements.

These are performed in sixteen ways:---

Prakírnaka, prakírnottara, nishanna, pársvánuvritta, úrmimárga , sarabhakrídita, sarabhapluta, tritála, báhyánuvritta, panchapáni, si mháyata, svádhúta, klishta, slághita, brimhita, pushpábhikírna.

Jumping like a monkey (*kapipluta*), jumping like a frog (*bhekapluta*), sudden jump (*ekapluta*), jumping with one leg (*ekapádapluta*), leaping like a cuckoo (*kokila-samchári*), dashing with its breast almost touching the ground (*urasya*), and leaping like a crane (*bakasamchari*) are the several forms of jumping.

Flying like a vulture (*kánka*), dashing like a water-duck (*várikánaka*), running like a peacock (*máyúra*) halt the speed of a peacock (*ardhmáyúra*), dashing like a mangoose (*nákula*), half the speed of a mangoose (*ardha-nákula*), running like a hog (*váráha*) and half the speed of a hog (*ardha- váráha*) are the several forms of gallop.

Movement following a signal is termed *nároshtra*.

Six, nine, and twelve *yojanas* (a day) are the distances (to be traversed) by carriage-horses.

Five, eight, and ten *yojanas* are the distances (to be traversed) by riding horses (*prishthaváhya*).

Trotting according to its strength (*vikrama*), trotting with good breathing (*bhadrásvása*), and pacing with a load on its back are the three kinds of trot.

Trotting according to strength (*vikrama*), trot combined with circular movement (*valgita*), ordinary trot (*upakantha*), middlemost speed (*upajava*), and ordinary speed are also the several kinds of trot (*dhárá*).

Qualified teachers shall give instructions as to the manufacture of proper ropes with which to tether the horses.

Charioteers shall see to the manufacture of necessary war accoutrements of horses.

Veterinary surgeons shall apply requisite remedies against undue growth or diminution in the body of horses and also change the diet of horses according to changes in seasons.

Those who move the horses (*sútragráhaka*), those whose business is to tether them in stables, those who supply meadow-grass, those who cook the grains for the horses, those who keep watch in the stables, those who groom them and those who apply remedies against poison shall satisfactorily discharge their specified duties and shall, in default of it, forfeit their daily wages.

Those who take out for the purpose of riding such horses as are kept inside (the stables) either for the purpose of waving lights (*nirájana*) or for medical treatment shall be fined 12 *panas*.

When, owing to defects in medicine or carelessness in the treatment, the disease (from which a horse is suffering) becomes intense, a fine of twice the cost of the treatment shall be imposed; and when, owing to defects in medicine, or not administering it, the result becomes quite the reverse, a fine equal to the value of the animal (*patramúlya*) shall be imposed.

The same rule shall apply to the treatment of cows, buffaloes, goats, and sheep.

Horses shall be washed, bedaubed with sandal powder, and garlanded twice a day. On new moon days sacrifice to *Bhútas*, and on full moon days the chanting of auspicious hymns shall be performed. Not only on the ninth day of the month of *Asvayuja*, but also both at the commencement and close of journeys (*yátra*) as well as in the time of disease shall a priest wave lights invoking blessings on the horses.

XXXI. THE SUPERINTENDENT OF ELEPHANTS.

THE Superintendent of elephants shall take proper steps to protect elephant-forests and supervise the operations with regard to the standing or lying in stables of elephants, male, female, or young, when they are tired after training, and examine the proportional quantity of rations and grass, the extent of training given to them, their accoutrements and ornaments, as well as the work of elephant-doctors, of trainers of elephants in warlike feats, and of grooms, such as drivers, binders and others.

There shall be constructed an elephant stable twice as broad and twice as high as the length (*áyáma*) of an elephant, with separate apartments for female elephants, with projected entrance (*sapragrívám*), with posts called *kumári*, and with its door facing either the east or the north.

The space in front of the smooth posts (to which elephants are tied) shall form a square, one side of which is equal to the length of an elephant and shall be paved with smooth wooden planks and provided with holes for the removal of urine and dung.

The space where an elephant lies down shall be as broad as the length of an elephant and provided with a flat form raised to half the height of an elephant for leaning on.

Elephants serviceable in war or for riding shall be kept inside the fort; and those that are still being tamed or are of bad temper shall be kept outside.

The first and the seventh of the eight divisions of the day are the two bathing times of elephants; the time subsequent to those two periods is for their food; forenoon is the time for their exercise; afternoon is the time for drink; two (out of eight) parts of the night are the time for sleep; one-third of the night is spent in taking wakeful rest.

The summer is the season to capture elephants.

That which is 20 years old shall be captured.

Young elephants (*bikka*), infatuated elephants (*mugdha*), elephants without tusks, diseased elephants, elephants which suckle their young ones (*dhenuká*), and female elephants (*hastiní*) shall not be captured.

(That which is) seven *aratnis* in height, nine *aratnis* in length, ten *aratnis* in circumference and is (as can be inferred from such measurement), 40 years old, is the best.

That which is 30 years old is of middle class; and that which is 25 years old is of the lowest class.

The diet (for the last two classes) shall be lessened by one-quarter according to the class.

The rations for an elephant (of seven *aratnis* in height) shall be 1 *drona* of rice, ½ *ádhaka* of oil, 3 *prasthas* of *ghi*, 10 *palas* of salt, 50 *palas* of flesh, 1 *ádhaka* of broth (*rasa*) or twice the quantity (*i.e.*, 2 *ádhakas*) of curd; in order to render the dish tasteful, 10 *palas* of sugar (*kshára*), 1 *ádhaka* of liquor, or twice the quantity of milk (*payah*) ; 1 *prastha* of oil for smearing over the body, 1/8 *prastha* (of the same) for the head and for keeping a light in the stables; 2 *bháras* of meadow grass, 2¼ *bháras* of ordinary grass (*sashpa*), and 2½ *bháras* of dry grass and any quantity of stalks of various pulses (*kadankara*).

An elephant in rut (*atyarála*) and of 8 *aratnis* in height shall have equal rations with that of 7 *aratnis* in height.

The rest of 6 or 5 *aratnis* in height shall be provided with rations proportional to their size.

A young elephant (*bikka*) captured for the mere purpose of sporting with it shall be fed with milk and meadow grass.

That which is blood-red (*samjátalóhita*), that which is fleshed, that which has its sides evenly grown (*samaliptapakshá*), that which has its girths full or equal (*samakakshyá*), that whose flesh is evenly spread, that which is of even surface on its back (*samatalpatala*) and that which is of uneven surface (*játadróniká*) are the several kinds of physical splendour of elephants.

Suitably to the seasons as well as to their physical spendour, elephants of sharp or slow sense (*bhadra* and *mandra*) as well as elephants possessed of the characteristics of other beasts shall be trained and taught suitable work.

XXXII. TRAINING OF ELEPHANTS.

ELEPHANTS are classified into four kinds in accordance with the training they are given: that which is tameable (*damya*), that which is trained for war (*sánnáhya*), that which is trained for riding (*aupaváhya*), and rogue elephants (*vyála*).

Those which are tameable fall under five groups: that which suffers a man to sit on its withers (*skandhagata*), that which allows itself to be tethered to a post (*stambhagata*), that which can be taken to water (*várigata*), that which lies in pits (*apapátagata*), and that which is attached to its herd (*yúthagata*).

All these elephants shall be treated with as much care as a young elephant (*bikka*).

Military training is of seven kinds: Drill (*upasthána*), turning (*samvartana*), advancing (*samyána*), trampling down and killing (*vadhávadha*), fighting with other elephants (*hastiyuddha*), assailing forts and cities (*nágaráyanam*), and warfare.

Binding the elephants with girths (*kakshyákarma*), putting on collars (*graiveyakakarma*), and making them work in company with their herds (*yúthakarma*) are the first steps (*upa-vichara*) of the above training.

Elephants trained for riding fall under seven groups: that which suffers a man to mount over it when in company with another elephant (*kunjaropaváhya*), that which suffers riding when led by a warlike elephant (*sánnáhyopaváhya*), that which is taught trotting (*dhorana*), that which is taught various kinds of movements (*ádhánagatika*), that which can be made to move by using a staff (*yashtyupaváhya*), that which can be made to move by using an iron hook (*totropaváhya*), that which can be made to move without whips (*suddhopaváhya*), and that which is of help in hunting.

Autumnal work (*sáradakarma*), mean or rough work (*hínakarma*), and training to respond to signals are the first steps for the above training.

Rogue elephants can be trained only in one way. The only means to keep them under control is punishment. It has a suspicious aversion to work, is obstinate, of perverse nature, unsteady, willful, or of infatuated temper under the influence of rut.

Rogue elephants whose training proves a failure may be purely roguish (*suddha*), clever in roguery (*suvrata*), perverse (*vishama*), or possessed of all kinds of vice.

The form of fetters and other necessary means to keep them under control shall be ascertained from the doctor of elephants.

Tetherposts (*álána*), collars, girths, bridles, legchains, frontal fetters are the several kinds of binding instruments.

A hook, a bamboo staff, and machines (*yantra*) are instruments.

Necklaces such as *vaijavantí* and *kshurapramála*, and litter and housings are the ornaments of elephants.

Mail-armour (*varma*), clubs (*totra*), arrow-bags, and machines are war-accoutrements.

Elephant doctors, trainers, expert riders, as well as those who groom them, those who prepare their food, those who procure grass for them, those who tether them to posts, those who sweep elephant stables, and those who keep watch in the stables at night, are some of the persons that have to attend to the needs of elephants.

Elephant doctors, watchmen, sweepers, cooks and others shall receive (from the storehouse,) 1 *prastha* of cooked rice, a handful of oil, land 2 *palas* of sugar and of salt. Excepting the doctors, others shall also receive 10 *palas* of flesh.

Elephant doctors shall apply necessary medicines to elephants which, while making a journey, happen to suffer from disease, overwork, rut, or old age.

Accumulation of dirt in stables, failure to supply grass, causing an elephant to lie down on hard and unprepared ground, striking on vital parts of its body, permission to a stranger to ride over it, untimely riding, leading it to water through impassable places, and allowing it to enter into thick forests are offences punishable with fines. Such fines shall be deducted from the rations and wages due to the offenders.

During the period of *Cháturmásya* (the months of July, August, September and October) and at the time when two seasons meet, waving of lights shall be performed thrice. Also on new-moon and full-moon days, commanders shall perform sacrifices to *Bhútas* for the safety of elephants.

Leaving as much as is equal to twice the circumference of the tusk near its root, the rest of the tusks shall be cut off once in 2½ years in the case of elephants born in countries irrigated by rivers (*nadija*), and once in 5 years in the case of mountain elephants.

XXXIII. THE SUPERINTENDENT OF CHARIOTS; THE SUPERINTENDENT OF INFANTRY AND THE DUTY OF THE COMMANDER-IN-CHIEF.

THE functions of the Superintendent of horses will explain those of the Superintendent of chariots.

The Superintendent of chariots shall attend to the construction of chariots.

The best chariot shall measure 10 *purushas* in height (*,i.e.,* 120 *angulas*), and 12 *purushas* in width. After this model, 7 more chariots with width decreasing by one *purusha* successively down to a chariot of 6 *purushas* in width shall be constructed. He shall also construct chariots of gods (*devaratha*), festal chariots (*pushyaratha*), battle chariots (*sángrámika*), travelling chariots (*páriyánika*), chariots used in assailing an enemy's strong-holds (*parapurabhiyánika*), and training chariots.

He shall also examine the efficiency in the training of troops in shooting arrows, in hurling clubs and cudgels, in wearing mail armour, in equipment, in charioteering, in fighting seated on a chariot, and in controlling chariot horses.

He shall also attend to the accounts of provision and wages paid to those who are either permanently or temporarily employed (to prepare chariots and other things). Also he shall take steps to maintain the employed contented and happy by adequate reward (*yogyarakshanushthánam*), and ascertain the distance of roads.

The same rules shall apply to the superintendent of infantry.

The latter shall know the exact strength or weakness of hereditary troops (*maula*), hired troops (*bhrita*), the corporate body of troops (*sreni*), as well as that of the army of friendly or unfriendly kings and of wild tribes.

He shall be thoroughly familiar with the nature of fighting in low grounds, of open battle, of fraudulent attack, of fighting under the cover of entrenchment (*khanakayuddha*), or from heights (*ákásayuddha*), and of fighting during the day and night, besides the drill necessary for such warfare.

He shall also know the fitness or unfitness of troops on emergent occasions.

With an eye to the position which the entire army (*chaturangabala*) trained in the skillful handling of all kinds of weapons and in leading elephants, horses, and chariots have occupied and to the emergent call for which they ought to be ready, the commander-in-chief shall be so capable as to order either advance or retreat (*áyogamayógam cha*).

He shall also know what kind of ground is more advantageous to his own army, what time is more favourable, what the strength of the enemy is, how to sow dissension in an enemy's army of united mind, how to collect his own scattered forces, how to scatter the compact body of an enemy's army, how to assail a fortress, and when to make a general advance.

Being ever mindful of the discipline which his army has to maintain not merely in camping and marching, but in the thick of battle, he shall designate the regiments (*vyúha*) by the names of trumpets, boards, banners, or flags.

XXXIV. THE SUPERINTENDENT OF PASSPORTS.

THE Superintendent of Passports shall issue passes at the rate of a *masha* per pass. Whoever is provided with a pass shall be at liberty to enter into, or go out of, the country. Whoever, being a native of the country enters into or goes out of the country without a pass shall be fined 12 *panas*. He shall be punished with the first amercement for producing a false pass. A foreigner guilty of the same offence shall be punished with the highest amercement.

The superintendent of pasture lands shall examine passes.

Pasture grounds shall be opened between any two dangerous places.

Valleys shall be cleared from the fear of thieves, elephants, and other beasts.

In barren tracts of the country, there shall be constructed not only tanks, buildings for shelter, and wells, but also flower gardens and fruit gardens.

Hunters with their hounds shall reconnoitre forests. At the approach of thieves or enemies, they shall so hide themselves by ascending trees or mountains as to escape from the thieves, and blow conch-shells or beat drums. As to the movements of enemies or wild tribes, they may send information by flying the pigeons of royal household with passes (*mudrá*) or causing fire and smoke at successive distances.

It shall be his duty to protect timber and elephant forests, to keep roads in good repair, to arrest thieves, to secure the safety of mercantile traffic, to protect cows, and to conduct the transaction of the people.

XXXV. THE DUTY OF REVENUE-COLLECTORS; SPIES IN THE GUISE OF HOUSEHOLDERS, MERCHANTS AND ASCETICS.

HAVING divided the kingdom (*janapada*) into four districts, and having also subdivided the villages (*gráma*) as of first, middle and lowest rank, he shall bring them under one or another of the following heads:---Villages that are exempted from taxation (*pariháraka*); those that supply soldiers (*áyudhíya*); those that pay their taxes in the form of grains, cattle, gold (*hiranya*), or raw material (*kupya*); and those that supply free labour (*vishti*), and dairy produce in lieu of taxes (*karapratikara*).

It is the duty of *Gopa*, village accountant, to attend to the accounts of five or ten villages as ordered by the Collector-General.

By setting up boundaries to villages, by numbering plots of grounds as cultivated, uncultivated, plains, wet lands, gardens, vegetable gardens, fences (*váta*), forests, altars, temples of gods, irrigation works, cremation grounds, feeding houses (*sattra*), places where water is freely supplied to travellers (*prapá*), places of pilgrimage, pasture grounds and roads, and thereby fixing the boundaries of various villages, of fields, of forests, and of roads, he shall register gifts, sales, charities, and remission of taxes regarding fields.

Also having numbered the houses as taxpaying or non-taxpaying, he shall not only register the total number of the inhabitants of all the four castes in each village, but also keep an account of the exact number of cultivators, cow-herds, merchants, artizans, labourers, slaves, and biped and quadruped animals, fixing at the same time the amount of gold, free labour, toll, and fines that can be collected from it (each house).

He shall also keep an account of the number of young and old men that reside in each house, their history (*charitra*), occupation (*ájíva*), income (*áya*), and expenditure (*vyaya*).

Likewise *Sthánika*, district officer, shall attend to the accounts of one quarter of the kingdom.

In those places which are under the jurisdiction of *Gopa* and *Sthánika*, commissioners (*prodeshtárah*) specially deputed by the Collector-general shall not only inspect the work done and the means employed by the village and district officers, but also collect the special religious tax known as *bali* (*balipragraham kuryuh*).

Spies under the disguise of householders (*grihapatika*, cultivators) who shall be deputed by the collector-general for espionage shall ascertain the validity of the accounts (of the village and district officers) regarding the fields, houses and families of each village---the area and output of produce regarding fields, right of ownership and remission of taxes with regard to houses, and the caste and profession regarding families.

They shall also ascertain the total number of men and beasts (*janghágra*) as well as the amount of income and expenditure of each family.

They shall also find out the causes of emigration and immigration of persons of migratory habit, the arrival and departure of men and women of condemnable (*anarthya*) character, as well as the movements of (foreign) spies.

Likewise spies under the guise of merchants shall ascertain the quantity and price of the royal merchandise such as minerals, or products of gardens, forests, and fields or manufactured articles.

As regards foreign merchandise of superior or inferior quality arriving thither by land or by water, they shall ascertain the amount of toll, road-cess, conveyance-cess, military cess, ferry-fare, and one-sixth portion (paid or payable by the merchants), the charges incurred by them for their own subsistence, and for the accommodation of their merchandise in warehouse (*panyágára*).

Similarly spies under the guise of ascetics shall, as ordered by the Collector-general, gather information as to the proceedings, honest or dishonest, of cultivators, cow-herds, merchants, and heads of Government departments.

In places where altars are situated or where four roads meet, in ancient ruins, in the vicinity of tanks, rivers, bathing places, in places of pilgrimage and hermitage, and in desert tracts, mountains, and thick grown forests, spies under the guise of old and notorious thieves with their student bands shall ascertain the causes of arrival and departure, and halt of thieves, enemies, and persons of undue bravery.

The Collector-general shall thus energetically attend to the affairs of the kingdom. Also his subordinates constituting his various establishments of espionage shall along with their colleagues and followers attend to their duties likewise.

XXXVI. THE DUTY OF A CITY SUPERINTENDENT.

LIKE the Collector-general, the Officer in charge of the Capital City (*Nágaraka*) shall look to the affairs of the capital.

A *Gopa* shall keep the accounts of ten households, twenty households, or forty households. He shall not only know the caste, *gotra*, the name, and occupation of both men and women in those households, but also ascertain their income and expenditure.

Likewise, the officer known as *Sthánika* shall attend to the accounts of the four quarters of the capital.

Managers of charitable institutions shall send information (to *Gopa* or *Sthánika*) as to any heretics (*Páshanda*) and travellers arriving to reside therein. They shall allow ascetics and men learned in the Vedas to reside in such places only when those persons are known to be of reliable character.

Artisans and other handicraftsmen may, on their own responsibility, allow others of their own profession to reside where they carry on their own work (*i.e.*, in their own houses).

Similarly merchants may on their own responsibility allow other merchants to reside where they themselves carry on their mercantile work (*i.e.*, their own houses or shops).

They (the merchants) shall make a report of those who sell any merchandise in forbidden place or time, as well as of those who are in possession of any merchandise other than their own.

Vintners, sellers of cooked flesh and cooked rice as well as prostitutes may allow any other person to reside with them only when that person is well-known to them.

They (vintners, etc.) shall make a report of spendthrifts and fool-hardy persons who engage themselves in risky undertakings.

Any physician who undertakes to treat in secret a patient suffering from ulcer or excess of unwholesome food or drink, as well as the master of the house (wherein such treatment is attempted) shall be innocent only when they (the physician and the master of the house) make a report of the same to either *Gopa* or *Stháníka*; otherwise both of them shall be equally guilty with the sufferer.

Masters of houses shall make a report of strangers arriving at, or departing from their houses; otherwise they shall be guilty of the offence (theft, etc.) committed during that night. Even during safe nights (*i.e.,* nights when no theft, etc., seems to have been committed), they shall be fined 3 *panas* (for not making such a report).

Wayfarers going along a high road or by a foot path shall catch hold of any person whom they find to be suffering from a wound or ulcer, or possessed of destructive instruments, or tired of carrying a heavy load, or timidly avoiding the presence of others, or indulging in too much sleep, or fatigued from a long journey, or who appears to be a stranger to the place in localities such as inside or outside the capital, temples of gods, places of pilgrimage, or burial grounds.

(Spies) shall also make a search for suspicious persons in the interior of deserted houses, in the workshops or houses of vintners and sellers of cooked rice and flesh, in gambling houses, and in the abode of heretics.

Kindling of fire shall be prohibited during the two middlemost parts of day-time divided into four equal parts during the summer. A fine of 1/8th of a *pana* shall be imposed for kindling fire at such a time.

Masters of houses may carry on cooking operations outside their houses.

(If a house-owner is not found to have ready with him) five water-pots (*pancha ghatínám*), a *kumbha*, a *dróna*, a ladder, an axe, a winnowing basket, a hook (such as is used to drive an elephant), pincers, (*kachagráhini*), and a leather bag (*driti*), he shall be fined ¼th of a *pana*.

They shall also remove thatched roofs. Those who work by fire (blacksmiths) shall all together live in a single locality.

Each houseowner shall ever be present (at night) at the door of his own house.

Vessels filled with water shall be kept in thousands in a row without confusion not only in big streets and at places where four roads meet but also in front of the royal buildings (*rajaprigraheshu*).

Any house-owner who does not run to give his help in extinguishing the fire of whatever is burning shall be fined 12 *panas*; and a renter (*avakrayi, i.e.*, one who has occupied a house for rent) not running to extinguish fire shall be fined 6*panas*.

Whoever carelessly sets fire (to a house) shall be fined 54 *panas*; but he who intentionally sets fire (to a house) shall be thrown into fire.

Whoever throws dirt in the street shall be punished with a fine of 1/8th of a *pana*; whoever causes mire or water to collect in the street shall be fined ¼th of a *pana*; whoever commits the above offences in the king's road (*rájamárga*) shall be punished with double the above fines.

Whoever excretes faeces in places of pilgrimage, reservoirs of water, temples, and royal buildings shall be punished with fines rising from one *pana* and upwards in the order of the offences; but when such excretions are due to the use of medicine or to disease no punishment shall be imposed.

Whoever throws inside the city the carcass of animals such as a cat, dog, mongoose, and a snake shall be fined 3 *panas*; of animals such as an ass, a camel, a mule, and cattle shall be fined 6 *panas*; and human corpse shall be punished with a fine of 50 *panas*.

When a dead body is taken out of a city through a gate other than the usual or prescribed one or through a path other than the prescribed path, the first amercement shall be imposed; and those who guard the gates (through which the dead body is taken out) shall be fined 200 *panas*.

When a dead body is interred or cremated beyond the burial or cremation grounds, a fine of 12 *panas* shall be imposed.

The interval between six *nálikas* (2 2/5 hours) after the fall of night and six *nálikas* before the dawn shall be the period when a trumpet shall be sounded prohibiting the movement of the people.

The trumpet having been sounded, whoever moves in the vicinity of royal buildings during the first or the last *yáma* (3 hours ?) of the period shall be punished with a fine of one *pana* and a quarter; and during the middlemost *yámas*, with double the above fine; and whoever moves outside (the royal buildings or the fort) shall be punished with four times the above fine.

Whoever is arrested in suspicious places or as the perpetrator of a criminal act shall be examined.

Whoever moves in the vicinity of royal buildings or ascends the defensive fortifications of the capital shall be punished with the middlemost amercement.

Those who go out at night in order to attend to the work of midwifery or medical treatment, or to carry off a dead body to the cremation or burial grounds, or those who go out with a lamp in hand at night, as well as those who go out to visit the officer in charge of the city, or to find out the cause of a trumpet sound (*turyapreksha*), or to extinguish the outbreak of fire or under the authority of a pass shall not be arrested.

During the nights of free movement (*chárarátrishu*) those who move out under disguise, those who stir out though forbidden (*pravarjitah*), as well as those who move with clubs and other weapons in hand shall be punished in proportion to the gravity of their guilt.

Those watchmen who stop whomever they ought not to stop, or do not stop whomever they ought to stop shall be punished with twice the amount of fine levied for untimely movement.

When a watchman has carnal connection with a slave woman, he shall be punished with the first amercement; with a free woman middlemost amercement; with a woman arrested for untimely movement, the highest amercement; and a woman of high birth (*kulastrí*), he shall be put to death.

When the officer in charge of the city (*nágaraka*) does not make a report (to the king) of whatever nocturnal nuisance of animate or inanimate nature (*chetanâchetana*) has occurred, or when he shows carelessness (in the discharge of his duty), he shall be punished in proportion to the gravity of his crime.

He shall make a daily inspection of reservoirs of water, of roads, of the hidden passage for going out of the city, of forts, fortwalls, and other defensive works. He shall also keep in his safe custody of whatever things he comes across as lost, forgotten or left behind by others.

On the days to which the birth star of the king is assigned, as well as on full moon days, such prisoners as are young, old, diseased, or helpless (*anátha*) shall be let out from the jail (*bandhanâgâra*); or those who are of charitable disposition or who have made any agreement with the prisoners may liberate them by paying an adequate ransom.

Once in a day or once in five nights, jails may be emptied of prisoners in consideration of the work they have done, or of whipping inflicted upon them, or of an adequate ransom paid by them in gold.

Whenever a new country is conquered, when an heir apparent is installed on the throne, or when a prince is born to the king, prisoners are usually set free.

Chanakya Niti

The Chanakya Niti of Kautilya is still very popular and some of the principles of Chanakya Niti are still practiced by some top corporate houses.

1. About the King and his Ideals

According to Kautilya the king should be all powerful and there should be no checks on his powers. But he should consult his ministers and respect the Brahmans. A king must be a highly educated and a cultured person, should have full control over his senses. He should save himself from his enemies, which are lust, anger, greed, vanity, haughtiness and love of pleasure. Service of the people should be the chief ideal of the king.

Another ideal before the king should be to save his people from external invasions and internal revolts. He should maintain a powerful army and a full treasury. He should be cunning as a fox, clever as a crow and brave as a lion.

2. About the King's Ministers

A king should appoint ministers both for assistance and consultation. It is difficult to run the government single-handed as single wheel cannot run a cart. These ministers should be men of high character and should be loyal, wise and brave. The king should consult his ministers, but he should not be a puppet in their hands, rather he should use his own judgment. The ministers should have team spirit and they should maintain perfect secrecy. Their meeting should be held at such a place where even the birds should have no access. A state' which cannot keep its secrets cannot last long.

3. About the Provincial Administration

From Kautilya we come to know that the Mauryan Empire was divided into many provinces, each province was further divided into many districts and each district had many villages in it. Each province was under the charge of a governor who generally belonged to the royal family.

4. About the Administration of Towns

The administration of the capital and other big towns of the Mauryan Empire were carried on in a very systematic way. Pataliputra, the capital of Chandragupta Maurya, was divided in four zones. Each zone was put in the control of a "Sthanik" who was assisted in the discharge of his duties by a large number of junior officers.

5. About the Espionage System

Kautilya lays a great emphasis on the espionage system. He is in favour of keeping a large number of spies by the king, because they are very necessary for the stability and progress of the state. The king could keep his hand on the pulse of the nation only if he knew what was going on in his empire. These spies could also help him in keeping a strict watch over the activities of the state officials. The king should keen spies in his neighboring countries too, because by doing this he can save his country from foreign attacks. According to Kautilya, women can prove better spies than men.

6. About Shipping

Important information that we get from Kautilya's Arthashastra is about Indian shipping. At each port a special officer was appointed whose main job was to control the movements of the ships and boats and to charge taxes from the merchants, travelers and fishermen. Generally all the ships and ferries belonged to the Government and shipping formed one of the chief sources of income of the Government.

7. About the Economic Condition of the People

Kautilya enjoins his king to improve the economic condition of his people because poverty is the chief cause of restlessness and rebellious spirit among them. So, whenever the king sees the signs of poverty he should at once take steps to root it out.

In this way we find that Kautilya's Arthashastra not only corroborates the information received from Megasthenes's 'Indika' but it also gives other useful information of great value.

The ***Arthashastra*** (Sanskrit: अर्थशास्त्र; IAST: *Arthaśāstra*) is an ancient Indian treatise on statecraft, economic policy and military strategy, written in Sanskrit. It identifies its author by the names "Kauṭilya"[1] and "Vishnugupta" (Viṣṇugupta),[2] both names that are traditionally identified with Chanakya (Cāṇakya) (c. 350–283 BCE),[3] who was a scholar at Takshashila and the teacher and guardian of Emperor Chandragupta Maurya, founder of the Mauryan Empire. The text was influential until the 12th century, when it disappeared. It was rediscovered in 1904 by R. Shamasastry, who published it in 1909. The first English translation was published in 1915.

Roger Boesche describes the *Arthaśāstra* as "a book of political realism, a book analysing how the political world does work and not very often stating how it ought to work, a book that frequently discloses to a king what calculating and sometimes brutal measures he must carry out to preserve the state and the common good."[5]

Centrally, *Arthaśāstra* argues how in an autocracy an efficient and solid economy can be managed. It discusses the ethics of economics and the duties and obligations of a king.[6] The scope of*Arthaśāstra* is, however, far wider than statecraft, and it offers an outline of the entire legal and bureaucratic framework for administering a kingdom, with a wealth of descriptive cultural detail on topics such as mineralogy, mining and metals, agriculture, animal husbandry, medicine and the use of wildlife.[7] The *Arthaśāstra* also focuses on issues of welfare (for instance, redistribution of wealth during a famine) and the collective ethics that hold a society together

EVOLUTION OF INDIAN ADMINISTRATION:

Indian 'Administration' traces its earliest known form to the tribal system which later emerges as a monarchical system. We gain a lot of knowledge about ancient Indian Administration from ancient religious and political treatises. In the early Vedic period there were many tribes who elected their own chiefs and he handled all their responsibilities and the administration of the tribes and the Sabha(Assembly of elders) and Samiti(Assembly of people) were the tribal assemblies. The chief protected the tribe but had no revenue system or hold over land thus wars were resorted to and the booty shared among the tribes.

The first form of the 'State' in India can be traced back to the times of Manu(original name Satyavrata) the first King and progenitor of mankind according to Hinduism.People were fed up with anarchy as there was no neutral judge/arbitrator in between to solve issues of society, and so they appointed Manu as King and paid service fees as taxes for looking after them and ensuring mutual benefit and justice to everyone in society owing to his wisdom and philosophical attitude & the King was divine and regarded as descended from God.

As per the Ramayana and Mahabharata/Later Vedic times it goes to portray the role of the King as the whole and sole of administration being helped by his principal officers who were the Purohit and Senani where the Purohit(Priest) wielded much more authority than the kshatriya(Warrior clan) kings. Other figures of administration were Treasurer,Steward,Spies and Messengers,Charioteer,Superintendent of Dices. This is also mentioned in the Manu Smriti and Sukra Niti.

No legal institutions were there and the custom of the country prevailed as the law and capital punishment was not practiced but trials took place where justice was delivered by the King in consultancy with the Priest and Elders at times. By the time Kautilya wrote the ArthaShastra the Indian Administrative system was well developed and the treatise of Kautilya gives a very first detailed account of the same. We will discuss that below.

KAUTILYA'S ARTHASHASTRA:

The Mauryan period was the era of major development in Indian Administration. Decentralisation was prevalent as the village units played a very important role as the base of administration since ancient times.Empires were divided into provinces,provinces into districts,districts into rural and urban centres for efficient administration.

Kautilya's ArthaShastra is a work on Varta (Science Of Economics) & Dandaniti(statecraft/Management Of State Administration) existing in the Mauryan rule. It was written sometime between 321 and 300 BC. It was retrieved in 1904 AD and published in 1909 AD by R. Shamasastry. It touches upon topics like functions of the chiefexecutive,hierarchy,bureaucracy,corruption,local administration,supervisory management,motivation, morale and job description.

The most noticeable aspect of the Arthashastra is its emphasis on Public Welfare even in an autocratic agrarian State. That is where its timelessness lies.

It is composed in the form of brief statements called Sutras and is compiled in 15 books(Adhikarnas),150 sections,180 chapters(prakarnas),6000 verses(sutras).

The 15 books could be classified under:

i) Concerning the discipline of economics and statecraft.
ii) Duties of government Superintendent.
iii) Concerning the Law
iv) Removal of thorns
v) Conduct of courtiers.
vi) Sources of sovereign State.
vii) End of six fold policy
viii) Concerning vices of the king and calamities that may arise as a consequence
ix) Work of an invader
x) Relating to a war.
xi) Conduct of a corporation
xii) Concerning a powerful enemy.
xiii) Strategic way of capturing a fort

xiv) Secret means like occult practices and remedies to keep of enemies or traitors.

xv) Plan of the treatise and thirty two methods of treating a subject.

Kautilya viewed the State as an institutional necessity for human advancement. According to him the State comprises of eight elements - King, Minister, Country, fort, treasury, army, friend and enemy. And State's prime function was to maintain law and order, punishing wrong doers and protecting subjects.

The empire was divided in to a Home Province (capital territory/administrative unit) under direct control of the central government and four to five outlying provinces (States),each under a viceroy responsible to the central government. The provinces possessed a good amount of autonomy in this feudal-federal type of organisation.Provinces were further divided into districts,districts into rural and urban centres with a whole lot of officials in charge at various levels.Departments to carry out execution of policy were created in all of these divisions with specialists dominating in the Mauryan era. Elites were preferred in job recruitment and the procedure for appointing is the same as it is practiced today. A centralised data bank of all government transactions and records were maintained in an organisation of the centre just like the cabinet secretariat and this performed audit and inspection functions of the three tiers of govt that is local, state and central.

This set up is very much similar to our present times where Union Territories and National Capital Territory are administrative units under Central rule where representative of the centre in the form of administrators/Lieutenant Governor appointed by the President rule the affairs under the direct supervision of the President & Central government.The states are under a governor(viceroy in olden times) appointed by and reporting to the President(King in olden times). The President is advised by his minister(s) and the sovereign power lies in the country's people. Also, the federal setup of powers given to states under the state list,and the district administration organisation and hierarchy. Audit mechanisms were in place and civil servants were recruited to perform the duties of policy implementation.

The King was head and his functions were military,judicial,legislative and executive,similar to modern state's functions of the President. And he was to be well equipped in all areas of study especially economics,philosophy,statecraft and the three Vedas. kautilya stated that whatever pleases the king only is to be avoided and only that which pleases the people is what needs to be followed. Kautilya stated that the king was like the Father and all the people/subjects of the country/empire were his children. That is how he is supposed to take care of them. This is conceptualised as Welfare State in Modern times.

Corruption was not tolerated at all and dealt with severely where the ill-earned money was confiscated. Kautilya had his own criteria for selection of officers for the same. Once basic qualifications were met he tested them on their attitude to piety,lucre/revenue,lust,fear. Those who completed this criteria of piety were appointed as judges/magistrates,and those who crossed the test of revenue became revenue collectors, and those pass the test of lust are appointed to the king's harem, The candidates passing the test of fear are appointed as king's bodyguards and personal staff. And those who pass all the tests are appointed as councillors.

There were two courts according to the Arthashastra called the Dharmasthya (civil cases court) where the matters are disposed off on basis of dharma,procedural law,conventions,royal decree ; and Kantakashodhana (criminal cases court) where accused is convicted on basis of testimony and eye witness of spies,etc. Similar to today's times where there are separate courts having the subject matter jurisdiction of civil or criminal issues.

Agriculture was the mainstay and taxes on the goods produced as well as its imports and exports were the source of revenue and the expenditure focused on public administration,national defense,army,salaries of govt. officials. Agriculture plays an important role even today in our country.

Therefore,as one can see Kautilya's arthashastra deals with a proper strategy and system of centralised autocracy with a welfare objective in mind before performing any function by the king and his ministers.

WEAKNESSES OF THE KAUTILYAN STATE:

i. Over charged with supervision - too much of checks and balances.

ii. Prominence on individuals instead of institutions.

iii. Fundamental mistrust of officials.

The Guptas carried forward the Mauryan legacy of administration in many respects.

LINKS BETWEEN KAUTILYAN ADMINISTRATION AND MODERN PERSONNEL ADMINISTRATION AND PUBLIC ADMINISTRATION:

1) Personnel Administration:

A system of recruitment was there and job description as well. Salaries were clearly spelled out of ministers and government officials. It also stated a view of job permanency and increment in salary/position(promotion) if the official concerned provided extraordinary service. Personnel were to be transferred from time to time as per Kautilya because it would avoid corruption and misappropriation of government funds. Removal and tenure of officials and ministers were at the pleasure of the King just like the Governor and Attorney General,etc. hold office at a term that specifies ' pleasure of the President'.

2) Public Administration:

The King is the sole source of authority and appoints and dismisses personnel and divides the work of govt. into different ministries under several ministers and officials. Kautilya stresses on the need for specialist and generalist personnel at different levels of administration with full accountability to the King,thus talks about division of labour and coordination between them for efficient administration. As discussed above there was a clear system of recruitment,pay,and terms and conditions of service very much resembling the modern State.

Modern state is more concerned about development whereas the Kautilyan model talks about collecting revenue and employing activities to help in expediting and ensuring revenue,so it talks mainly of control instead of development.
It talks about local self government that very much resembles a precursor to the Modern State local self government model.

Kautilya's Arthashastra is more about political science that is how to conduct State affairs rather than focusing on the philosophy that underlies it. He is very practical in his approach with a strict focus on amorality(no moral principles or religious diktat) so that the King's rule & administration are neutral without offending anyone, and also on rationality and an organised as well as efficient way of running a system with a greta deal of focus on accoutability and honesty and vigilance.

MUGHAL ADMINISTRATION:

The Mughal administration was the most organised and long lasting and has even carried on to to the modern times. The reason for this stability was the long lasting more than 3 centuries rule of the Mughal sultanat. Akbar was the architect of this system since his grandfather and father Babur and Humayun respectively had their hands full with battles and socio-economic uncertainties leaving little time for administrative activities.

A very detailed,reliable and brilliant account of Akbar's empire,society and administration is given in the famous detailed document/text by Abul Fazl titled Ain-i-Akbari(Constitution Of Akbar).

The Mughal administration did carry forward a lot of the earlier traditions in political and administrative matters already existing in India as mentioned above but they upheld greater centralisation and a rigid structure without paying much interest to social services of health and welfare as also morals as compared to the Mauryan rulers. Their's was an islamic state and right from the principles of government,church policy,taxation rules,departmental arrangements to the titles of officials all was imported wholesale from the Perso-Arab crescent of khalifs of Iran and Egypt. However, even though the recruitment was mainly based on caste and kin they also did recognise merit and talent and did open up the civil services for Hindu people. It's source of revenue was taxation on land and agriculture and was highly urbanised. In the lower levels like of politics,village and lower levels of officials the Indian usage and customary practices were allowed whereas at the court/darbar and in higher official circles the foreign imported model of policy prevailed.

The sovereign was the king who was paternalistic and he had supreme authority over everything. He did have a number of ministers to help,advise and assist him in the discharge of his functions,out of which the more important were four - the Diwan who was in charge of revenue and finance,the Mir Bakshi at the head of the military department,the Mir Saman in charge of factories and stores, and the Sadr-us-Sudur who was the head of the ecclesiastical and judicial department.

Administration was based on coercion in the name of the King by the officials. The main functions of the officials were to maintain law and order,safeguard the King's interests from internal uprising and revolts,defend and extend boundaries of the empire and collect revenue and taxes.

Every officer of State held a mansab (official appointment of rank and profit and expected to supply certain number of troops for State military service),thus the bureaucracy was essentially monetary in character. The officials ranged from Commanders of 10 to 10000 and were classified into 33 grades. Each grade carried a certain rate of pay,from which its holder was to provide a quota of horses,elephants,etc and the State service was neither hereditary nor was it specialised. Grading system is practiced even today in recruitment matters.

The pay was received in form of either cash or jagir for a temporary period from which he could collect revenue equivalent to his salary. Thus,the jagirs though having no hold over the land extracted revenue at their whims and fancies from the land.

The Army of the Mughal empire must be understood in terms of the Mansabdari system. And apart from that there were the knights who were called the gentleman troopers and owed exclusive allegiance to the King. The cavalry was the most important unit,the infantry was made up of townsmen and peasants and the artillery with guns and the Navy.

The corruption within the army where the soldiers payed more allegiance to the immediate boss rather than the king proved to be its undoing and thus could be easily overpowered by the Marathas during the time of Jahangir.

The Policing system of the Mughals was entrusted to village headman's and subordinates in villages and to Kotwals in cities and towns. And at the district level the faujdars took over. It was a precursor to modern policing system of India.

The administration at the Centre was personal and paternal and operated with a fair degree of efficiency as long as the King kept an eye and controlled effectively. The two highest officials were the Vakil and the Wazir of which the former was higher in position and functioned as the regent of the State and maintained over all charge of the same.

The Wazir was the head of the revenue department and was known as Wazir when he acted as a Prime Minister.

Chief Diwan supervised revenue collection and expenditure and was the head of the Government's administrative wing supervising work of all high officials. All provincial diwans and their subordinates reported to him and he signed and authorised all government transactions. A Musatufi audited the income and expenditure of the government and the Waqia Navis kept a record of all important farmers.

The Khan-i-Saman was the high steward of the royal expenditure and the Mir-i-Bakshi who was the paymaster General of the empire.

The Provincial or State Administration was also known as Subahs(for states/provinces) and was headed by the Subedar or the

Governor. He was appointed by the King and was given a office insignia and instrument of instructions which defined the powers, functions and responsibilities. As executive head he was in charge of provincial administrative staff and ensured law and order there. He also handled local civil intelligence agencies and controlled the local zamindars and contained their political influence.

Provincial Diwan was appointed by the central diwan and was next in the line of importance after the Provincial governor. He appointed kiroris and tehsildars to extract revenue from the ryots in time. He also exercised audit functions and had full control over public expenditure. He was assisted in office by the Office Superintendent, head accountant, treasurer and clerk.

The provincial Bakshi performed the same function as the central bakshi.

The Sadr and Qazi were two officers at provincial level who were sometimes united in the same person but the Sadr was basically a civil judge but did not handle all civil cases and the Qazi was concerned with civil suits in general and also with criminal cases.

DISTRICT AND LOCAL ADMINISTRATION UNDER MUGHAL RULE:

The Subah/Province was further divided into Sarkars which were of two types. One was ruled by officers appointed by the emperor and those under the tributary rajas. Each Sarkar was headed by Faujdar,he was the executive head who had policing and military functions and could surpass the provincial rulers to speak directly to the imperial government.

The Amalguzar was in charge of the revenue and the other head of the Sarkar. The Kotwal did the policing. The qazi performed the judicial duties. The Sarkars were further divided into parganas and the parganas further divided into Chaklas headed by officials called Chakladars. Qanungos kept the revenue records and the Bitikchi was the accountant and Potdar was the title of the treasurer.This was the hierarchy for a sound and efficient administration

Akbar kept the land revenue at 1/3 and Todar Mal brought

in reforms as in a standard system of land revenue collection that included survey and measurement of land,classification of land based on its fertility and fixing the rates.

Justice was administered based on the Quranic Law as the Mughal state was a Muslim State. Fatwas were issued when required and ordinances by the emperor. The principles of equity were followed and the Emperor's interpretations only was allowed till the point it did not run contrary to the sacred laws.

LEGACY OF BRITISH RULE IN POLITICS AND ADMINISTRATION - INDIANIZATION OF PUBLIC SERVICES:

Though many of Indian administrative and political features evolved post 1947 but there still are certain features that we can see as a legacy of the British times continuing for the sake of its efficient practices and no other better alternative to the same till now.

Under the charter (official paper) of the British crown the East India Company came to India with the sole objective of making profit through commercial exchanges. The established factories here and for their protection set up a small base of soldiers. They started looking for monopolising their profits in India as her market and resources were unmatched. This led to the initial tussle with Bengal Nawab and the event of Battle of Plassey paved the way for the same. The company officials convinced the company directors that if they interfered and got a say in local policy making in india then it would lead to a lot of profit and surplus.

Lord Cornwallis developed the Civil Services Code and so he is aptly known as the Father Of Modern Civil Services. He regularised and specified the office of the District Collector and estabilished the office of the District judge. This helped the company achieve a well organised personnel administration through which control over territories/provinces in India could become more comprehensive.

Lord Wellesley's rule period saw the emergence of the office of the Chief Secretary(1799). The doctrine of Subsidiary Alliance was an aggressive policy that resulted in the active interest of company officials in political and administrative affairs of local kingdoms governed by local Rajas. The early 1800s could be seen as an era where company officials focused all their strategies in gaining interference rights in political,commercial and military policies of local kingdoms for their profit.

The office of the Commissioner and sectional arrangement in the Secretariat saw the light of the day under Lord Bentick's rule. Under the Charter Act of 1833, the Governor General of Bengal was appointed as the Governor General of India and policy formulation was centralised for all territories under the company at the council of the Governor General Of India(Head of the British Administration In India). Also there was an estabilishment of communication between the Governor general's office which was the headquarter and its various field units and formal units of organisation. 1844 established 4 departments of Finance, Home, Foreign and Military as well as a little later on under Lord Dalhousie the setting up pf Post and Telegraph Services, Railways and Public Work Departments. The Doctrine Of lapse theory of Dalhousie very blatantly spelled out the objective of the company in India as to have absolute control over the policy process in Indian States.

Thus all these establishments and policies helped the English to set up a strong base in India along with rights of revenue by means of strong organisational infrastructures and institutions, and interference in legislation and policy making even in the remotest of areas.

The Revolt of 1857 then shook up this system and that led to the end of the British East India Company's rule in India. The govt of India Act 1858 passed in the British parliament led to the company's dissolution and all powers transferred to the British Crown which then created an India Office in India and a Secretary Of State post was established with Indian governance and policy formulation matters. the Governor General was converted to Viceroy General of India(chief administrator of the British Crown in India) who implemented the policies devised by the India office which actually only had the role of passing on orders of the British

Parliament. Military was reorganised and more higher caste officials were appointed at the higher levels and lower level occupied by lower caste as well as Europeans held the titular positions in the army. All this was done to avoid another mutiny so that communication is minimum considering the caste biasedness prevalent in India.

So,in short the British East India Company paved the way for the British government to enter. As soon as the Company outlived its utility,it was removed and the British govt. directly entered the Indian domain.

Impey devised a civil procedure code and Macaulay devised the Indian Penal Code, Contract Act and Indian Council Act.The enactment of the Criminal procedure Code by the British Parliament in the 1860's brought immense joy to the local rajas and people as they thought that now all the English officers would function under a code of conduct and there will be uniformity in treatment. There was also formulation of Arms act, Vernacular press act, Relationship codes, Transfer rights,etc. Thus, this era of late 1800's could be seen as one that was dedicated to establishing a legal environment for the smooth functioning of the British officials as they felt that no rules and regulations earlier led to the situation of disarray and sepoy mutiny/revolt.

There was also the demand of indianisation of the Civil services that was first totally occupied by Europeans and was causing a lot of discontent among Indians and Indian associations. Thus,for this purpose the Aitchison Commission recommended the induction of 25% Indians into the ICS,but this only remained on paper.The Islington Commission was appointed in 1912 and its repirt,submitted in 1915 recommended a scheme of 2 entry paths to the civil services. One was for insuring induction of natives of India through competitive exams and the other exam for superior ICS and Home services preliminary exam to be conducted in England was open to all. The Civil services was under the control of the Secretary Of State.

The Govt. Of India Act in 1919, created the All India Services replacing the imperial civil services format. This act also advocated the setting up of Public Service Commissions in India. The provincial civil services were under the control of the provincial governments.

Lee Commission and the Royal Commission on superior civil services specially recommended for the establishment of central services. Subordinate services were advocated for removal from the classification of civil services and transferred to the regional levels for conducting exams and filling up of positions only by Indians. So,basically it was a system to prevent Indians from entering the higher civil services as everybody could not afford to go to England for training and exam purpose and the lower levels were more approachable and attainable by the Indians.Also English as a compulsory language offered little scope of success for non-westernised Indians.On the recommendation of the Lee Commission,the first Public Service Commission was setup at Allahabad in 1925. The Lee Commission recommended a 40-40 percent of Europeans and Indians to fill up the superior ICS and the rest 20% to be filled up with promotions from the provincial Indian sub ordinate services. thus he advocated 60% Indians. This led to the Britishers losing interest in joining the services as they feared a monopoly of Indians and so the number of Indians in the services increased gradually.The Govt. Of India Act 1935 provided for the setting up of federal Public service commissions and also recommended for similar institutions at the state levels. This was the realisation of giving the All India Service an Indian flavour and towards the Indianisation of Civil Services.

Portfolio system was introduced in the Central Secretariat under Lord canning and arrangement of departments under Lord Mayo,Lord Lytton and Lord Ripon. Tenure arrangement was introduced under the Secretariat staffing scheme of Lord Curzon in 1905.

A special mention needs to be made here of the administrative systems/features passed on:

Judicial administration system of the Mughal period still exists in Indian administration.

REVENUE ADMINISTRATION & DISTRICT ADMINISTRATION UNDER BRITISH RULE:

After the battle of Buxar ended with the treaty of Allahabad,the company obtained "Diwani" rights from Shah Alam II and was legally authorised to issue dastaks in the name of the King thus paving the way for the company officials to enter revenue assessments and collection duties.

This very event began the evolution of the system of district arrangement that we see today. The District Collector's office was established in 1772 and it played a leading role in stabilising the company's hold over the revenue at local levels. 1780 saw the establishment of a Revenue Board created as the apex advisory body for suggesting scheme of Land Revenue Settlement. This is where we see the shift of the company majorly from commercial activities to administrative control in india. The revenue Board's recommendations culminated into : Permanenet Settlement Act in Bengal,Orissa and areas of Assam, Ryotwari arrangement in Presidencies of Maharashtra and Bombay, Mahalwari system in areas under the control of North India.

LOCAL SELF GOVERNMENT UNDER BRITISH RULE:

This term originated during British rule. Lord Ripon is called the father of local self government in India but was unable to push for major reforms. They lacked autonomy and gradually declined by way of establishment of local civil and criminal courts,revenue and police organisations,increased communication, and starting of the Ryotwari system where peasants paid directly and individually instead of collectively or under the zamindar.Panchayats maintained the local social order according to the socio-political norms prevailing.

The Montague Chelmsford reform in 1919 made it a transferred subject under the dyarchy that led to the establishment of a number of panchayats in all villages to have a proper and efficient local self government/administration as well as revenue collection for the British but was still under the total control of the District collector and red tapism and corruption plagued it and funds crunch was always there as a deliberate attempt by the British to stranglehold the provincial Indian governments from having control over them and so had to depend on the centre/British government for everything.

So, the local self government though had control over certain aspects but in the others it was just a pawn of the British government for their colonial benefits.

Corruption in Administration: Evaluating the Kautilyan Antecedents

Corruption is not a recent phenomenon. It has precisely been defined as a deviant human behaviour, associated with the motivation of private gain at public expense[1] and, as such, has persisted for centuries. Corruption promotes illegality, unethicalism, subjectivity, inequity, injustice, waste, inefficiency and inconsistency in administrative conduct and behaviour.[2] It destroys the moral fabric of society and erodes the faith of the common man in the legitimacy of the politico-administrative set up.

There are several references to the prevalence of official corruption in ancient India.[3] But the text that provides an elaborate description of the menace is the *Arthashastra* of Kautilya. This sophisticated and detailed treatise on statecraft is essentially prescriptive or normative in nature, belonging to a genre of literature that suggests what the state ought to be and not what it really was. Nevertheless, one should realise that norms are prescribed only when digressions or abnormalities exist. This confirms the fact that corruption was rampant enough in ancient India to necessitate expert advice on how to tame it.

Kautilya was a sagacious minister in the Kingdom of Chandragupta Maurya (324/321–297 Before the Common Era). He expressed his views on a range of issues including state, war, social structures, diplomacy, ethics, and politics. He believed that "men are naturally fickle minded" and are comparable to "horses at work [who] exhibit constant change in their temper". This means that honesty is not a virtue that would remain consistent lifelong and the temptation to make easy gains through corrupt means can override the trait of honesty any time. Similarly, he compared the process of generation and collection of revenue (by officials) with honey or poison on the tip of the tongue, which becomes impossible not to taste. 6 Based on such sweeping, albeit questionable, generalisations about the nature of human beings, he prescribed a strict vigil even over the superintendents of government departments in relation to the place, time, nature, output and*modus operandi* of work. All this is perhaps indicative of widespread corruption in the Kingdom's administration at various levels.

Corruption is so obvious, and yet so mysterious. Even Kautilya reflected serious concerns about opacity in the operations of the world of the corrupt. Illegal transactions were so shrouded in mist that he compared embezzlers to fish moving under water and the virtual impossibility of detecting when exactly the fish is drinking water. 8 He also noted that while it is possible to ascertain the movements of bird flying in the sky, it is difficult to gauge the corrupt activities of government officials.

During Mauryan times, superintendents were the highest officials, a position they received for possessing the desired 'individual capacity' and adequate 'ministerial qualifications'. Given the general emphasis of Kautilya on observing ethics and morality in relation to the functioning of a state, it seems the selection process would have involved not just a scrutiny of the educational attainments but also the right kind of aptitude for the job including traits of honesty and impartiality. This shows that despite the greatest care taken in recruiting officials, corrupt persons made their way into the system.

Kautilya was a great administrative thinker of his times. As he argued, too much of personal interaction or union among the higher executives leads to departmental goals being compromised and leads to corruption. This is because human emotions and personal concerns act as impediments to the successful running of an administration, which is basically a rule-based impersonal affair. Similarly, dissension among executives when team effort is required results in a poor outcome. Kautilya suggested that the decline in output and corruption can be curbed by promoting professionalism at work. The superintendents should execute work with the subordinate officials such as accountants, writers, coin-examiners, treasurers and military officers in a team spirit. 12Such an effort creates a sense of belonging among members of the department who start identifying and synchronising their goals with the larger goals of the organisation, thereby contributing to the eventual success of the state.

Kautilya provides a comprehensive list of 40 kinds of embezzlement. In all these cases, the concerned functionaries such as the treasurer *(nidhayaka)*, the prescriber *(nibandhaka)*, the receiver *(pratigrahaka)*, the payer *(dayak)*, the person who caused the payment *(dapaka)* and the ministerial servants *(mantri-vaiyavrityakara)* were to be separately interrogated. In case any of these officials were to lie, their punishment was to be enhanced to the level meted out to the chief officer *(yukta)* mainly responsible for the crime. After the enquiry, a public proclamation *(prachara)*was to be made asking the common people to claim compensation in case they were aggrieved and suffered from the embezzlement. Thus, Kautilya was concerned about carrying the cases of fraud to their logical conclusion.

The Arthashastra states that an increase in expenditure and lower revenue collection *(parihapan)*was an indication of embezzlement of funds by corrupt officials. Kautilya was sensitive enough to acknowledge the waste of labour of the workforce involved in generating revenues. He defined self enjoyment *(upbhoga)* by government functionaries as making use of or causing others to enjoy what belongs to the king. He was perhaps alluding to the current practice of misusing government offices for selfish motives such as unduly benefitting the self, family members, friends and relatives either in monetary or non-monetary form which harms the larger public good.

Kautilya was also not unaware of corruption in the judicial administration. He prescribed the imposition of varying degrees of fines on judges trying to proceed with a trial without evidence, or unjustly maintaining silence, or threatening, defaming or abusing the complainants, arbitrarily dismissing responses provided to questions raised by the judge himself, unnecessarily delaying the trial or giving unjust punishments. This shows that there were incidents of judicial pronouncements being biased, favouring one party to the detriment of others. In an atmosphere of corruption prevailing in the judicial administration as well, Kautilya perhaps wanted to ensure that the litigants are encouraged and given voice to air their legitimate grievances. He expected judges to be more receptive to the complaints and be fair in delivering justice.

Kautilya prescribed reliance on an elaborate espionage network for detecting financial misappropriation and judicial impropriety. Spies were recruited for their honesty and good conduct.They were to keep a watch even over the activities of accountants and clerks for reporting cases of fabrication of accounts (avastara). On successful detection of embezzlement cases, Kautilya advocated hefty fines to be imposed apart from the confiscation of ill-earned hordes. If a functionary was charged and proved even of a single offence, he was made answerable for all other associated offences related to the case. Since taxes paid by the people are utilised for their welfare, any loss of revenue affects the welfare of the society at large. This is precisely the reason why Kautilya explicitly argued that the fines imposed should be "in proportion to the value of work done, the number of days taken, the amount of capital spent and the amount of daily wages paid".

The threat of fines being imposed and subsequent public embarrassment do deter judicial officials, to some extent, from resorting to corrupt practices. But Kautilya was proactive in laying down traps to catch public functionaries with loose morals and inclination to resort to bribery or seek undue favour. The strategy he prescribed was for secret agents to take a judge into confidence through informal channels and ask him to pronounce judgments favouring their party in return for a payment. If the deal was fixed, the judge was treated as accepting the bribe and prosecuted accordingly.

Interestingly, Kautilya also dealt with the concept of whistleblowers. Any informant *(suchaka)* who provided details about financial wrongdoing was entitled an award of one-sixth of the amount in question. If the informant happened to be a government servant *(bhritaka)*, he was to be given only one twelfth of the total amount. The former's share was more because exposing corruption while being outside the system was more challenging. But in the case of *bhritakas*, striving for a corruption free administration was considered more of a duty that was ideally expected of them.

Kautilya also warned at the same time about providing wrong information or not being able to prove the accusations. He advocated either monetary or corporal punishment for such informants so that the tool could not be misused for settling personal scores and harassing genuine officials. If an informant himself were to backtrack on the assertions he made against the accused, Kautilya suggested the death penalty for him. This provision was not only draconian, but would have effectively discouraged whistleblowers. While such provisions would certainly make people think twice before levelling accusations, the threat of capital punishment was too harsh to help people root out the corrupt.

In an atmosphere of all round corruption, honesty becomes a virtue and not a desired duty. Kautilya argued for advertising the cases of increase in revenue due to the honest and dedicated efforts of the superintendents by giving rewards and promotions. Bestowing public honour creates a sense of pride and boosts the motivation and morale of honest officials. They act as role models for ideal youngsters who wish to join the administration and serve the state.

Kautilya also proposed a number of measures to avoid cases of corruption arising at all. Several positions in each department were to be made temporary. Permanency for such positions was to be reserved as an award granted by the king to those who help augment revenue rather than eating up hard earned resources. 25 Kautilya also favoured the periodic transfer of government servants from one place to another. 26 This was done with the intention of not giving them enough time to pick holes in the system and manipulate it to their advantage.

Kautilya wrote that "dispensing with (the service of too many) government servantsconducive to financial prosperity". 27 This is not only because of the reduction in expenditure on salary but rightsizing the bureaucracy also results in faster decision making and the transaction of government business without unnecessary delay and red tape. This effectively reduces the scope for bribery in particular and corruption in general.

It is interesting to note that the superintendents could not undertake any new initiative (except remedial measures against imminent danger) without the knowledge of the king. Kautilya, therefore, laid emphasis on some kind of an accountability mechanism. Apart from using the services of spies for unearthing cases of fraud, Kautilya also talked about an intra-departmental, self-scrutinising mechanism under the headship of chief officer *(adhikarna)* to detect and deter imminent cases of corruption.

The *Arthashastra* of Kautilya thus shows that the ancient system of governance and administration was quite contemporary in operational guidelines when dealing with corruption. It also quite convincingly demonstrates that corruption is not an exclusive feature of modern times alone. The fact that the menace has survived and thrived through the ages speaks volumes about its endurance. Governments of all historical eras have recognised its illegality and devised legal instruments to tackle the problem, but they have not been able to overcome its spread as well as acceptability in society. If corruption has persisted through centuries, what is it that has stopped administrative systems from eradicating it?

Was Kautilya right in his generalisation that 'humans are fickle-minded'? The majority would disagree. Interestingly, however, even Kautilya, despite having such an understanding of human nature and behaviour, never used it to justify corruption. Rather, he realised its inevitabilitybut chose to remain positive and committed to root it out in the administration through elaborate and strict measures. This is the real significance of the *Arthashastra* as far as the issue of corruption in contemporary times is concerned.

Chanakya's Views on Administration

By
Dr. Shrikant Yelegaokar

FIRST EDITION

LAXMI BOOK PUBLICATION
258/34, Raviwar Peth,Solapur-413005
Mobile : +91 9595359435

Rs: 250 /-

Chanakya's Views on Administration

Dr. Shrikant Yelgaokar

ISBN –978-1-329-08280-9

Published by,
Laxmi Book Publication,
258/34, Raviwar Peth, Solapur,
Maharashtra, India.

Contact No. : +91 9595 359 435
Website : http://www.isrj.org
Email ID : ayisrj@yahoo.in

www.ingramcontent.com/pod-product-compliance
Ingram Content Group UK Ltd.
Pitfield, Milton Keynes, MK11 3LW, UK
UKHW041944190726
13854UKWH00004B/1775

9 781329 082809